ADVENT 2019 ABQ

JUSTIN EDGAR

Published by White Blackbird Books, an imprint of Storied Publishing

Permission requests and other questions may be directed to the Contact page at www.storied.pub.

These entries were written by members of City Presbyterian Church, Albuquerque, New Mexico.

CONTENTS

INTRODUCTION

This Lenten Devotional is for you. We're going through the days and weeks of Lent (and then one week after).

Each week is broken up into an Introduction of the theme for the week, the daily devotional reading, and then a weekend reflection. There are spots where we've dropped in various quotations from books, poems, and music.

This book will work through the various aspects of worship in our lives. These moments form a pattern, not only for our worship, but for our whole lives.

May the Lord bless you during this season.

WEEK ONE

THE KEEPING OF TIME

Justin Edgar

So teach us to number our days
that we may get a heart of wisdom
~ Psalm 90:12

As my kids have gotten older, gathering around a table has become harder. We don't just do it around our farm table in our dining area anymore, but we grab time at Chick-fil-A and Chipotle or maybe even standing around our kitchen island with food in hand. When we gather, we pray, and then I ask them, "Ok, so what are your hummers and bummers?" For orientation, a hummer is something you are rejoicing, and a bummer is something you are lamenting. It has become a habit for our family. It is, in a sense, the way we mark time. We practice hummers and bummers in an attempt to number our days. It becomes a stake to mark the Lord's goodness, and to mark the reality of living in the "not yet" world of sin and brokenness. All is not right with the world, but God is good — "All-The-Time, All-The-Time, God is good."

Marking time is something every culture does. We remember important moments in our story. Events that have shaped and formed us as a people. What holidays are important in the American story? We remember the troops, the vets, the presidents, significant people in history, our independence. We also market other holidays, which become the "High-Holy" days of the calendar — Christmas and Easter; Halloween and Valentine's Day. These days are a merging of traditions and commercialism. There is a push to buy things. This is how we mark time. Again, every culture does it.

The church calendar is an attempt to mark time by something else, namely Jesus. Pastor and Theologian Greg Thompson says the following: "In a world where history has no meaning, where it is just the tale of the victors or the scholars, a world where things emerge and dissipate, a world where nations are here today and gone tomorrow, we believe that history progresses towards an end, a goal. That goal and that end is Jesus and His kingdom. So we mark our days by the birth, life, death, ascension and pentecostal blessing of Jesus."

The church calendar has two primary cycles, and between them is something we call ordinary time. First there is the incarnational cycle. It centers on the brith of Jesus. It begins with Advent, moves into Christmas and ends with the season of Epiphany, which highlights Jesus going public. The second cycle is the paschal cycle, which centers around the death and resurrection of Jesus. This season includes Lent, Holy Week and Easter ending with Pentecost and the blessing of the Spirit.[1]

We mark time with a different calendar, because we want to be shaped by a different story. Yes we are Americans, and yes we buy stuff, but we don't want that to be our story and our song. We want to be the song that Jesus is playing in the world. So we mark time by this story.

Lent is one season in this story. It is 40 days. It moves from Ash Wednesday to Easter. Lent is a time marked by repentance and renewal. During this 40 days, practicing Lent, means we mark this time by self-examination, confession of sin and repentance because we are not yet the people God has made us to be. But we also do so in hope, because of the resurrection of Jesus. The shaping power of this 40 days is being vulnerable to the reality that we are a sinful and broken people in need of God's renewing grace and love. So we practice confession. We embrace forgiveness.[2] We may practice self-denial in some tangible way. We may also add some new practice into our life during this season. We don't do this to practice our own righteousness or win some sort of prize for self-denial. We do it to enter the story. We do it because we are lovers who need to be rehabituated out of our other loves. We love glory. We love victory. We love progress. We love acquisitions. We don't love losing. We don't love struggling. We don't love lamenting. Lent forms us and shapes us to see that winning comes from losing. Progress comes through struggle. Lament and confession are part of the story living in this time between times, between Jesus' ascension and second coming. We practice Lent, so we may be renewed. So we might experience God by the Spirit renewing us in faith and repentance.

The Psalmist in Psalm 90 asks the Lord to teach him to number his days, so he might gain wisdom. Wisdom is this way of being in the world, where we do what is right and good at the right time and in the right way. We practice Lent, so we might gain wisdom, so we might be in our worlds living right, doing right at the right time and in the right way.

God, help us to practice this Lenten season. Help us to confess. Help us to lament. Help us to repent. And bring us to Easter Sunday, renewed and refreshed as your people living in your world, numbering our days and walking in wisdom. Amen.

—Justin Edgar

WEDNESDAY

FORMED IN AND BY THE DUST

Justin Edgar

For he knows our frame;
he remembers that we are dust.
~ Psalm 103:14

One of the most powerful moments of my ministry life was the first time I imposed ashes on the foreheads of God's people. There was an older saint who ambled down to the front. She was in her late 80's, I think. She had this intense and earnest look in her eyes, and I spoke the words: "Dear Sister, remember you are dust, and to dust, you will return." The reality of death met me in the words that I spoke as I imposed ashes on a real person who knew death was more near now than 30 years earlier. It overwhelmed me. It humbled me.

Ash Wednesday forms and shapes us to be a people to remember our frame. We practice it, because we want to remember that we are not God, and that we have limits. We are not in control of our own lives. We are dust, and to dust we will return. In a world that worships the young, that sterilizes death and thinks at some level that our progress will save us from the inevitable... the ashes, the words and the practice places us back into the hands of God. And the Psalmist takes great comfort, because of God's intimate knowledge of our frame. He lives and sits into that frame. God knows we are dust. What a tender thought. He knows we are fragile, frail, weak, needy, limited by breath, time and space. He knows we are dust. This life is a vapor, and Ash Wednesday reminds us that this life is a gift. We have no guarantees our life will extend into tomorrow. But we do have a guarantee that God knows this about us, and because He knows this, He will uphold us. Through His resurrected life He will renew and re-enliven us, breathing into us the breath of life. That breath will resurrect our dry bones and bring this dust new life.

Almighty God, you have created us out of the dust of the earth: Grant that these ashes may be to us a sign of our mortality and penitence, that we may remember that it is only by your gracious gift that we are given everlasting life. (Book of Common Prayer)

DUST

David Michael Bruno

Arms firmly held to breasts
Fingers touching chin
Head bowed, head cocked
Eyes tightly locked

Carved by a scythe
Hunched like a wound
Unmoved, despair
Under cloak of blackened hair

Quiet in a shell
Unvoiced troubled words
A whisper of a breath
Dread of life and of death

Guilty. Guilty. Guilty.

Rusted then crushed
Upon a human life of tin
Iron-weight of holiness on sin

How blessed when

Bent limbs unbend
Hands reach down
Knees touch dirt to crawl
To earth all hearts must fall

To earth's dust returns our fouled and fearful years
From that very dust we cleanse His feet with our tears

David Michael Bruno. "The Rabbit Room." The Rabbit Room Theres No Right or Wrong In Art Comments, 24 May 2016, rabbitroom.com/2016/05/dust/.. "The Rabbit Room." The Rabbit Room Theres No Right or Wrong In Art Comments, 24 May 2016, rabbitroom.com/2016/05/dust/.

THURSDAY

YOU BECOME WHAT YOU BEHOLD

Justin Edgar

*They followed worthless idols
and became worthless themselves.*
~ Jeremiah 2:5

*And we all, with unveiled face, beholding the glory of the
Lord, are being transformed into the same image from one
degree of glory to another. For this comes from the Lord who
is the Spirit.*
~ 2 Corinthians 3:18

My buddy posted on my wall on Facebook: "Wherever you
stare, so you will steer." This captures the thoughts of the
two verses above. We become what we behold. What holds
your gaze? What captures your imagination? What do you

find yourself daydreaming about, fantasizing about, scheming and strategizing about? It could be self-improvement, a relationship, a problem, a promotion, a future event or date (getting married, graduation), a dream, success, your phone. Where are you staring?

I know success can capture my heart. I want it, dream about it, scheme how to get it. And when I am overwhelmed with that, I gaze at escape: The next place to go, conference to attend, golf course to play or friend to visit. What holds your gaze? Whatever holds your gaze, has your love and captures your imagination. Your rituals and rhythms will be shaping you to grasp hold of it.

Tim Keller says:

> "*unless you learn how to behold the glory of Christ, you aren't living the Christian life...to behold the glory of Jesus means that we begin to find Jesus beautiful and if we don't behold Him then something else will be beheld and that thing will rule our lives.*"[1]

What's crucial to remember about this is that we are all as Jack Johnson says, "just people watching." Have you ever done that, people watched? What do you do when you people watch? You set yourself up in a spot where there are lots of people — an airport, a mall, an outdoor space. You don't look at anything else, and if you do it is just a passing glance. So your phone, your book, your paper is just something in front of you, so you don't look weird. And then you watch, you behold. This says something about the practice. To people watch, you can't be beholding other things with any kind of focus. You have to keep your gaze out there. You have to set yourself up where people are. You can chill on a bench at Central Park, but maybe not Alvarado Park. There is purpose, place, posture and position. You practice it. This is true for us and our beholding of Jesus. You must have a purpose, you must make a place and then position or posture yourself to do it. There are practices of beholding. Just like there are practices in beholding success, there are practices in beholding Christ. Where is your stare? Wherever it is, is where you will be steered.

God, I stare at all sorts of worthless things. Things hold my gaze. Why do I get so easily distracted when I try to gaze at you? Why can't my habits hold? I'm always captivated by the shiny, new thing. Forgive me my lack of staring. Let me see your beauty and let me be captivated. Arrange my heart so it is aimed at you. Renew my practices and presence of those practices, so I might be changed from one small degree of glory to the next. Amen.

FRIDAY

PRACTICES OF LOVE

Justin Edgar

So here's what I want you to do, God helping you: Take your everyday, ordinary life—your sleeping, eating, going-to-work, and walking-around life—and place it before God as an offering. Embracing what God does for you is the best thing you can do for him. Don't become so well-adjusted to your culture that you fit into it without even thinking. Instead, fix your attention on God. You'll be changed from the inside out. Readily recognize what he wants from you, and quickly respond to it. Unlike the culture around you, always dragging you down to its level of immaturity, God brings the best out of you, develops well-formed maturity in you.
~ Romans 12:1-2 (The Message)

I'm a golfer, kind of. I mean I play golf, and I have been

moderately ok at it. I shot my lowest consistent scores when I worked at a golf course. This isn't surprising, because golf during that time was always before me. I mean, I looked at a course all day. But I didn't just behold it in that way. I also put a stick in my hand and practiced and played it. I got lessons from the pro, because they were free and he was a friend. The place coupled with the practice made me a better golfer.

As part of this, I wanted to change my swing. So, I went to work everyday, with my instructor, and at the range. The pro gave me drills, embodied things to work on to go about changing it. Early on those drills would over-emphasize and compensate aspects of the new swing, so that by practicing and ingraining into my "muscle-memory" my swing change would take root. With those tools and practices, I changed my swing, and my scores.

Paul tells the church in Rome, that transformation comes from both offering our bodies, all of us, and fixing our attention God. These two things come not just from beholding it, but come from practicing it. We must practice offering our bodies and we must practice fixing our attention. We don't just think about it, and boom, we're changed. As part of this, we recognize there are other things that want our bodies and our attention as well. When I worked at the golf course, I could give my body and attention to golf in ways I couldn't if I did not work there. I needed to give my body and attention to it if I was going to see transformation. If Christ will be formed in us, our bodies and attention are required. And the way we give our bodies and attention, is by practicing the drills that overcompensate for all that we learn out there, and train us to live in new ways here. These practices are practices of love, means of God's grace where by the practicing of them, God shapes and forms us through them.

God, help me to offer by body and fix my attention upon you. Help me to practice my faith, both to find those practices that affix my attention and capture my body, and then give me the godly discipline to offer my body to do them again and again. Attune my attention upon you in these practices, so that I feel your rhythm and dance to it, harmonize with it, knowing your good love and grace. Amen.

WEEKEND

FOR THE LIFE OF THE WORLD

Justin Edgar

In this way we are like the various parts of a human body.
Each part gets its meaning from the body as a whole, not
the other way around. The body we're talking about is
Christ's body of chosen people. Each of us finds our meaning
and function as a part of his body. But as a chopped-off finger
or cut-off toe we wouldn't amount to much, would we?
So since we find ourselves fashioned into all these excellently
formed and marvelously functioning parts in Christ's body,
let's just go ahead and be what we were made to be, without
enviously or pridefully comparing ourselves with each other,
or trying to be something we aren't.
~ Romans 12:3-4

Have you thought about how your arm serves the rest of

your body? I remember this horror movie called *Body Parts*, where this guy loses his arm in an accident, and he gets an arm transplant. The arm he gets is the arm of a killer, and that arm starts operating on its own and for its own desires over and against the rest of the man and his body. It is a funny thought really. Your arm operating without awareness of the body. Your arm doing its own thing.

Paul instructs the church that the offer of our bodies is for the health and well-being of the whole. It is for others that we offer our bodies and affix our attentions on God. It isn't just for me, as an arm. It is for the whole. The practices that form Jesus in us, are practices not just for me as the arm, but for the whole body. I spend time in prayer, and practice hospitality, and confess my sin, and pass the peace, and receive a benediction for the life of the world. The arm serves the body, by typing devotions and lifting forks and serving bread and wine.

Spirit, help me to be an arm that serves the rest of the body. Help the practices that feed my body and soul and form Jesus in me to be practices that bless not just me, but bless others. Remind me that these spiritual disciplines are for your people and your world. Amen.

A LITURGY FOR THE KEEPING OF HOLY LENT

Justin Edgar

Leader: As the king cake has been eaten
And party clothes have been lain aside,
As we put on ash and grave clothes
And mourn, lament and cry.

People: May we keep a Holy Lent.

Leader: As we make promises
And then fail to do what we wish,
As we give up all the sweet things
And only eat fried fish.

People: May we keep a Holy Lent.

Leader: As we stammer and stumble
And fall again upon our knees,

As we groan and fumble
And only fake our way through these things.

People: May we keep a Holy Lent.

Leader: As we await the resurrection
Waving palms and singing Hosanna,
As our dirty, stinking feet are washed
And we march out in Friday darkness.

People: May we keep a Holy Lent.

Leader: Let us sing your Alleluias
For you have done great things!
As you have raised us from the grave!
And clothed us with robe and ring!

All: Let us keep a Holy Lent!

WEEK TWO

THE SABBATH

Justin Edgar

As they continued their travel, Jesus entered a village.
A woman by the name of Martha welcomed him and
made him feel quite at home. She had a sister, Mary, who
sat before the Master, hanging on every word he said.
But Martha was pulled away by all she had to do
in the kitchen. Later, she stepped in, interrupting
them. "Master, don't you care that my sister has abandoned
the kitchen to me? Tell her to lend me a hand."
The Master said, "Martha, dear Martha, you're fussing
far too much and getting yourself worked up over nothing.
One thing only is essential, and Mary has chosen it—it's the
main course, and won't be taken from her."
~ Luke 10

The better thing...what is the better thing?

In his book called *The Common Rule*, Justin Whitmel Earley shared about leaving the mission field in China to pursue law, because he felt God leading him to help the disenfranchised. He went to law school, got employed and worked hard, and then one night found himself in the hospital suffering from anxiety and a panic attack. He said,

"We have a common problem. By ignoring the ways habits shape us, we've assimilated to a hidden rule of life: The American Rule of Life."[1] The American Rule of Life centered on work, busy-ness and success, and Justin became habituated by it. Even though he knew the Gospel and loved Jesus, he found himself over working and not entering any sort of rest.

Martha is at home in the kitchen. She is a perfection helper, and finds herself embittered when her sister, a free-spirited romantic perhaps feels no need to follow her or the culture by working in the kitchen while the men visit in the other room. She has been habituated by a story both her own and her people's. She does what she does. She works. She cooks. She serves. She cleans up. And she gets bitter. Thinking she has Jesus ear on such traditional matters, she groans to him. And He does what Jesus does, flips it on its head, and says to Martha that Mary has chose the essential thing —resting in the presence of Jesus, and it won't be taken from her to serve in the kitchen.

What is forming you in regards to your rest? More American need sleeping aids than every before. More suffer from anxiety. More have panic or manic episodes. For al our technological advancement, we seem to have less freedom not more. We all have been formed by working rest and rest-less work. We can't sow down for fear of what we might feel or discover, and we can't slow down for fear of missing out, and we can't slow down because there is too much to do, and if we don't do it who will. And there is Jesus, telling us, I've done it all. Stop. Sit. Rest a while. It is the essential thing. Sabbath is essential. It was made for us. This week, we reflect on the formative power of Sabbath rest.

MONDAY

EXODUS 20:8-11

Lorrie Whatley

Imagine your entire life consumed with doing chores—chores that you detested, chores without a weekly allowance, and chores that in no way benefited you or your family. From morning to night. Day after day. Week after week. Year after year. Chores, chores, chores! No time for recreation. No time for school. No time for church activities.

Then suddenly one day it was determined that you no longer had to do those chores. What would be the perfect way to celebrate?

To a far greater extent, that would be similar to what the Israelites had experienced in the Old Testament when God gave them the 10 Commandments. They and their ancestors had been slaves in Egypt. They made mud-bricks from morning to night, day after day, for 400 years—all to strengthen Pharaoh's kingdom. Then, through an amazing turn of events (that we now call "Crossing the Red Sea"), God rescued them from slavery in Egypt.

With that backdrop in mind, imagine what the Israelites must have been thinking the first time they heard what we now call the 4th Commandment:

> *Remember the Sabbath day, to keep it holy. Six days you shall labor, and do all your work, but the seventh day is a Sabbath to the Lord your God. On it you shall not do any work, you, or your son, or your daughter, your male servant, or your female servant, or your livestock, or the sojourner who is within your gates. For in six days the Lord made heaven and earth, the sea, and all that is in them, and rested on the seventh day. Therefore the Lord blessed the Sabbath day and made it holy.*

I wonder what the Israelites thought and felt when they heard those words? Perhaps they were in awe: Seriously.... we no longer need to work 24/7 *for a slave master?* We now have 6 days a week to do our own work? And one day every week we get to celebrate our freedom by AVOIDING work altogether (without the fear of being beaten or put to death) —a weekly holiday to focus on our new Master—the gracious One who rescued us from slavery!

Imagine their joy (and probably some confusion) the first time they celebrated Sabbath Day: Celebrating their freedom from slavery in Egypt by taking a holiday from their work in order to worship the One who rescued them. A day of REST & worship. Now that's a fitting way to celebrate!

While the Israelites' deliverance from Egypt was worthy of weekly remembrance, this was merely a glimpse when compared to an even greater rescue to follow: God would rescue all His children from spiritual slavery to sin which carried the penalty of eternal death. He accomplished our freedom and secured our eternal salvation through the death & resurrection of Jesus Christ. This salvation does NOT depend on our work for God, but the work that God accomplished for us.

Are we in awe at that our God rescued us from a slavery even worse than Egypt? and granted us eternal salvation-- even greater than Crossing the Red Sea?

What's the fitting way for us to celebrate our freedom and demonstrate that we are RESTING in God's provision for our salvation, rather than our own efforts?

> *Come to me, all who labor and are heavy laden, and I will give you rest. Take my yoke upon you, and learn from me, for I am gentle and lowly in heart, and you will find rest for your souls. For my yoke is easy, and my burden is light."* Matthew 11:28-30

Lord, remind us to celebrate our freedom from slavery to sin by RESTING FROM our efforts to earn salvation and RESTING IN what You accomplished for us. May that be evident in our lives by serving you joyfully every day of the week!

TUESDAY

MARK 2:23-28

Jeremy Warren

Have you ever found yourself getting lost in the means and you forget that there was even an end to reach? This almost happened to me this past week. As a side hustle-freelance graphic designer, finding clients and keeping my business active is crucial.

Well, I just turned down a prospective client. They wanted me to re-do their website on a platform that I have little experience with. I know I need to know the platform, so I was thinking that I would binge watch YouTube for a few hours and figure the thing out...

And then I can be the yes man I want to be with clients, as well as continue growing my business's profit. But in further conversations with some friends who are experts, it quickly became clear that I would spend about **100 hours** of working on this site, and that was not including the mass amounts of learning needed first!

There were so many red flags about the project, but I was trying to justify the means to get to the end. Here's the breakdown: The means are knowing and doing the necessary skills and tools to complete any given task. The end is doing quality work for a client to make decent money on the side. But my vision of the end in this situation was being clouded by an overwhelming, stressful, and unattainable means to reach that end. This client could have ended my company. I would have gotten burned out, while I frustrated my client with a snail-like pace of accomplishing tasks and showing progress.

The means were just not allowing me to reach the end. So I turned them down! I can take on so many more projects and clients in those 100 hours, that my ends are now possible to reach again.

In Mark 2:23-28 we meet Pharisaical tension between the Law and Jesus. The Law was incredibly necessary for the people of God as they followed Moses through the wilderness. And it stayed foundational to life with God...until Jesus came. In that Law, it stated that God's people are not to work on the Sabbath because it was a day of rest. What we often see with the Law and the Pharisees is that legalism lurks closely behind every action. But there are means to an end that we must notice here.

There is a day of rest for followers of God because God saw it was valuable to rest. He rested. There is a day of rest to keep perspective that God is still the one who holds everything together. We can take a day off when we could be productive or make money. But, the end purpose of a day of rest is not for it to be a rule, but for it to be a GIFT!

God has penciled-in refreshment and recharging for us because he knew it would be good and enjoyable for us. It is a holy gift that provides us time with Him, time with His Body, and, of course, a Sunday afternoon nap (queue the

Instagram post of the guy sleeping on the couch with his baby sleeping on his chest - the epitome of joyous Sunday Afternoon Naps.) Rest. *"The Sabbath was made for man, not man for the Sabbath."* Let's not lose site of the end goal while we filter through the grain fields of the means.

Lord, may we learn how to rest well. May you teach us in this busy culture how to truly, holistically, and righteously worship you on the Sabbath. And may we know how to slow down enough to enjoy the gift that you have provided of resting in and on the Sabbath. In the name of the Father, the Son, and the Holy Spirit we cry out to you. Amen.

WEDNESDAY

PSALM 127:2

Denise Riggs

"One month sabbatical?! Can I cancel my support for that month too?" Our friend laughed at his joke and nervously, so did we. My husband and I work for a missions organization that requires we raise our own salaries and our friend is a financial supporter. Though we are mostly sure he was indeed joking, it still stung deeply. There were traces of guilt and shame we felt for needing to take a sabbatical after 10+ years on staff. Sabbatical for us meant taking time away from the regular work demands of ministry and spending more time just resting in the Lord. People don't really celebrate your rest after the age of three. You can probably get away with it for a few more years but eventually it starts to look like weakness. Even on the day of Sabbath we can sometimes find glory in 'serving' others. We become glory hogs. "Look at all I can do!"

Before we began our sabbatical, many thoughts about it crossed my mind...my own thoughts and what others might think. Why would you need to take time away from your work? Are you really that tired? That needy? Burnt out? Yes, the truth is a resounding yes. I am needy. I cannot do it all. I was not made to. None of us were. I have not done a good job of resting well. If even God who after six days of doing good work (and it was very good!) took a sabbath, then I should not only find more value in rest but also start to understand just how integral He created it to be in our lives. Obviously, month long sabbaticals won't always be ideal, in fact they're pretty rare.

Nonetheless, we should still take sabbath seriously and regularly. As a parent, when I see that my child is exhausted and a hot mess or on the brink of becoming undone I know he/she needs rest. I don't then ask them to do more and push them to work harder. On the contrary, I do my best to stick to schedules and routines that allow them and even force them to rest. To be still. Of course my father in Heaven is going to ask the same thing of me.

Including rest in our routines is crucial. We weren't created to do it all and without proper rest we can't even do all that we were created for. Lack of rest has serious consequences. It affects everything from our mood to our long-term health and functioning. Is it a weakness? Yes! Is it a blessing? Absolutely. It makes me feel a little giddy inside and slightly spoiled when I think about God telling me to rest. But he is just that good! This life is not about me. And even though it may sometimes feel like it, not everything depends on me and that is freeing. The glory is always all his.

Heavenly Father, thank you for telling me to rest. Would you continually remind me of all the ways I can rest in you? I pray that I would remember you don't need me to do it all but you created me to know you, to love you, live with you, and glorify you. Amen

THURSDAY

MATTHEW 12:1-14

David Breidenbach

A pastor friend of mine recently opined that, as a society, we only really observe and generally agree on a limited number of the Ten Commandments, as given by God to His people. Murder, stealing, bearing false witness, and honoring father & mother are among those that are a "given" on the list. If you or I murder, steal, or bear false witness against somebody we go to jail. Covetousness, adultery, and having no other gods tend to have grey areas that society, all too often, finds ways to forgive, accept and, in some cases, encourage. However, there is one Commandment that, almost across all societal norms, we actually celebrate and revere when it is broken! By not observing God's Commandment of Sabbath most will receive an "at-a-boy" and possibly get a raise for working so hard! This is not God's plan for you and certainly it is not something to be celebrated and rewarded.

However, God did not give us Sabbath as just another way to observe the Law and demonstrate allegiance to Him. He gave us Sabbath for our spiritual, physical, and mental health and well-being. The Pharisees who confronted Jesus saw his "working" for a meal and healing on the Sabbath as breaking the Law. While Jesus (God in the flesh!) demonstrated that Sabbath is, indeed, the time to step away from those things that distract, consume, and draw you away from dwelling on the things of God, he also demonstrated that you may still exercise those things that are healthful, compassionate, loving, and point to all we have been given in God's provision of grace, love, and mercy!

If you're still not convinced of God's provision in not working on the Sabbath; consider this: Supposedly, studies have revealed that Jehovah's Witnesses generally live 11 years longer than the average expected life span. (Please note that I am in no way endorsing Jehovah's Witnesses.) Coincidentally, if you add up one Sabbath day per week, over the course of an average human lifespan, it equals 11 years! That is a direct return on investment in God's command to Sabbath! It's almost as if He planned it that way. To God be the glory!

Gracious and loving Father, forgive us our desire to trust in our own abilities and productivity more than in what you promise is your provision. Grant us genuine faith to recognize that Your economy is not our economy and that obedience to Your will is to our benefit and well-being. May we rest in you and be satisfied in the sufficiency of your Word and may we find comfort and refreshment by seeking to dwell in your presence. Amen.

FRIDAY

JOHN 5:1-16

Taeler Larsen

"Do you want to be healed?"

I find it comforting when I know exactly what my day holds and when I have specific times set aside for work, rest, and play. Ideally, I start my day with coffee. This is accompanied by a time of meditation. This is then followed by a time of attempting to play piano and sing. After that, I go to whichever job I am working that day. I end my day somewhere between 4:30-5:00pm so I can come home and get dinner together. I enjoy eating an early dinner. Evenings are for friends and/or books. The next day this cycle repeats itself.

Of course, my ideal day often gets disrupted by extra work, car breakdowns, phone calls from family, spontaneous adventures with my husband, and all sorts of miscellaneous tasks. And when my schedule gets disrupted, I get *angry*. So often I have been the individual who sees the lame man walking and yells at him for carrying his mat on the Sabbath. Because it disrupts those things that *I* control.

It's often only when I am weak, after being physically ill for an extended period of time or after being emotionally beaten-down, that I hear Jesus' question, "Do you want to be healed?" and I weakly answer back, "God, is that even possible at this point?". It is usually in moments such as this —in my weakness and doubt—that God has shown up and begun works of healing in my life that I never believed possible anymore.

God, help me to not merely live a righteous life... but to have a wondrous sense of your beauty. Forgive me for my selfish desire for control over the time you have given me. Let my heart be ready to experience You whether it be in my time of "rest" or my time of "work" or my time of "play". Let me see that my true rest and enjoyment are found in You alone.

WEEKEND REFLECTION

GOOD NEWS! YOU'RE A SINNER AND LENT IS HERE

Will Willimon[1]

Lent is that time when we all-too-worldly ones learn and relearn the great scandal that lies at the heart of the Christian faith—Christ came to save sinners, only sinners.

Much of the time we get away with the fiction that we are, after all, down deep, rather nice people who have no need of salvation. We know we may not be the best people in the world, but we are not the worst. We are making spiritual progress, lifting ourselves (by ourselves) out of the muck and mire of what once was called "sin."

And then comes the church smearing ashes upon our foreheads, forcing us to our knees in confession, teaching us to say, "Lord, have mercy, Christ have mercy upon us sinners."

That's not something many of us want the church to do anymore.

Years ago, we had the popular spiritual writer Thomas

More come to speak at Duke. More is a very nice man who believes that we are all rather nice people, and if we just learn to think about ourselves as he thinks about us, we would be ever so much happier. On the way out of More's rather vague self-help homily, I encountered a woman who said to me, "I'm so glad next week is Ash Wednesday."

Glad for Ash Wednesday? I pressed for more. She responded, "You don't know me that well, but I was the victim of sexual abuse by a relative when I was a young teenager. Spent years in therapy trying to get over it. Pop-spirituality and feel-good religion were just no help to me. That's why I'm glad that we are coming to that time of the year when the church makes us put all the injustice, sin, blood and guilt on the altar and forces us to look at it and let God deal with it."

Rejoice. It's Lent. This is when the poor, old, bumbling church courageously reminds us of the joy of letting go of our illusions about ourselves. We offer our lives not to a God with high standards of conduct, but to a God who loves us as we are and forgives the worst in us.

My favorite theologian, Karl Barth, said that "only Christians sin." He meant that only Christians know the joy of a God who forgives and thus can be frank about their sin. There is a sense in which awareness of God's grace comes before, and not after, true and honest repentance. The person who doesn't know a gracious God can never be truly honest about sin.

Sit quietly for a moment and dare to delve into today's horrific headlines – or, if you really want to be bold, consider your own selfish, cheating little heart — and you are liable to be overwhelmed, defeated by guilt and shame. An honest look at yourself leaves you only one option: self-deceit.

That's when Christians give thanks that, in Jesus

Christ, we know the truth about God. We know that God loves, forgives, and embraces sinners.

The great Christian apologist C. S. Lewis was once asked why so many people who are atheists are such really good people.

Lewis responded, "Well, they have to be good, don't they? If you don't believe in a God who forgives, you are damned to unrelenting goodness."

In our lamenting of our sins, there is also room for joy. In the gospel reading for Ash Wednesday, Matthew 6:16-17, Jesus instructs us (strangely) that when we fast, when we repent of our sin, we are not to show sad, remorseful faces and make a big deal of our mournful repentance. Jesus tells us that we are to prepare ourselves as if for a party. We are to rejoice that the God whom we presumed to be our enemy is really our best friend.

Give thanks that the God whom we presumed to be unwilling to do business with sinners such as us has embraced us, forgiven us, even died for us sinners, only sinners.

"Why should men love the church?" asks T. S. Eliot. "Because she tells them of sin and death and other unpleasant facts of life they would as soon forget."

We don't think of Ash Wednesday as one of the happiest, most joyful services of the year, but maybe we should.

WEEK THREE

BENEDICTION

Justin Edgar

*Blessed be the God and Father of our Lord Jesus
Christ, who has blessed us in Christ with every
spiritual blessing in the heavenly places, even as he
chose us in him before the foundation of the world, that we
should be holy and blameless before him.*
~ Ephesians 1

Benediction is the "good word." Do you need a good word?
My friend Chris needed it. Chris is a church planter. He
took over a church that he didn't start, and worked as its
pastor for nearly five years. His church closed last year. It
was sad to see. I know Chris loved this church. I know he
and his wife prayed for it. I know he worked hard to help it
become a flourishing church. I know he had people who

loved him and it, and yet it still closed. At a meeting with a group of pastor's, Chris shared his confidence that God had chosen him to do this work, and that although it was hard he was ok with doing it. He talked about God's love and grace in his seeming failures. At the end, another pastor stood up and said a "good word" over Chris. He just told Chris that we were all proud of him. It's true. We were... are. He also said to Chris that God rejoiced over him with loud singing. Alleluia! This is true. He does. We all need the "good word" from our Holy God pronounced over us. We all need to hear God's loud singing voice, quieting us with love. In that moment Christ was given a type of benediction. And the hope is that it aims him towards the good life of Jesus and His kingdom and flourishing in it.

This week, we start looking at the end of our worship service—the practice of benediction. We start here, because the benediction forms and shapes us first in the Gospel. We have been blessed with every spiritual blessing in Christ Paul says. Because we are in Christ, we have the merits of Christ, the benefits of Christ. We have the medals around our neck, medals that we didn't win on our own accord. Medals won for us by Jesus. This is Gospel truth. You have been blessed. The end leads to the beginning. Because knowing the end, shapes how we begin and live in the middle.

Benediction also shapes us for the end. It is like a laser pointer. It points us towards something. We walk out in the good word of God aimed at the world. Shot out of the building of the church to be the church in our homes, neigh-borhoods, jobs and cities. It also points us towards the end of the story. Blessed to be a blessing to walk in God's forever blessing now and in new heaven's and new earth. This is a "good word" is the shaping power of God's people.

MONDAY

Brooks Anderson

The Lord spoke to Moses, saying, "Speak to Aaron and his sons, saying, Thus you shall bless the people of Israel: you shall say to them, The Lord bless you and keep you; the Lord make his face to shine upon you and be gracious to you; the Lord lift up his countenance upon you and give you peace.
"So shall they put my name upon the people of Israel, and I will bless them."
~ Numbers 6:22-27

Lent is a time that most people think of as dark, somber, and having to go without. For some it may trigger feelings of guilt and shame, as they self-examine their hearts. Others try to give something up to "check a box" or "to seem spiritual," but in truth they don't want to be inconvenienced.

One of my children gave up "only" vanilla ice cream one year. Anything else felt like too much. Another has given up all sweets multiple years in a row, but that child doesn't even have a sweet tooth. They just like the feeling of other's being impressed that they could give up something "so hard".   Both get the idea of lent, but not the essence of what God wants to do in us, in this time.

Staying in the mental and emotional state of lent takes work. Work our society is not comfortable with. We like to swing the pendulum between total hopelessness with no purpose or a false sense of seeming to have it all together and living the dream.

I sat mediating on this passage in Numbers with our newborn daughter taking a sunbath in the window of our hospital room. She was the perfect picture of total rest and peace, even as her jaundice numbers were medium high, and we were praying they would go down. I had learned with my 3rd child, that sunlight on the face brings healing for jaundice. The face is something sacred. It reflects the inner state of the soul. It tells family lineage and a person's personal history. Laugh lines, culture, scars, sadness, pain, peace, joy, all reflect in our face.

How beautiful a picture then, in a time of repentance, sadness over our sins and having to do without, to remember the Lord gives us the healing Sonshine. Warmth that draws our face and turns our whole body in His direction. We are sometimes more comfortable with the idea of an angry, exacting, distant God, then one that's gentleness brings healing to the imbalances in our soul and who's warmth open's us up to peace and rest. Healing being done just by receiving. Not striving, doing or cloaking ourselves in "spiritual piousness" to seem worthy. For this Lenten season, as we live in the land of enchantment (and sunshine) I pray we would each turn our face daily to feel and heal in the Sonshine.

Lord, help us to bask in the light and the heat of your Son's shining face ever pressed towards us. May we practice this holy Lent with the knowledge of your perfect love shining down on us, responding with devotion in all our giving and all our receiving. Amen.

TUESDAY

EPHESIANS 3:17-21

Cole Larsen

As I write this, I find myself trying to fix a lot of things: my job, my finances, my patients and the people in my life. I certainly don't feel benediction or "the state of being blessed" as one of the online definitions described it. The to-do list is always growing, and my resources (time, empathy, money, ability) are oh so limited. It feels as if a mountain is piling on top of me and I'm not even making a dent in the coming avalanche.

As I reflect on this passage, it reminds me just how little I esteem God. Sometimes he likes to knock us out of our comfort zone and remind us who we are. As Eugene Peterson put it in his interpretation, "I ask him to strengthen you by his Spirit—not a brute strength but a glorious inner strength—that Christ will live in you as you open the door and invite him in. And I ask him that with both feet planted firmly on love, you'll be able to take in with all followers of

Jesus the extravagant dimensions of Christ's love. Reach out and experience the breadth! Test its length! Plumb the depths! Rise to the heights! Live full lives, full in the fullness of God."

I think one of the reasons I've always loved The Message is the level of passion conveyed. Here was a man who was so deeply in love with Christ. He knew his own depravity, and couldn't help but proclaim the grace he had been given. I think that's where it starts. Recognizing we don't have it together and clinging to Christ for dear life. Then remembering that he is waiting expectantly for us to desire his invasion into our lives. We only begin to appreciate God's bigness by contemplating it, and then realizing we can't even comprehend it. Only then, do our eyes begin to open to the blessings He desires to pour out on us.

Jesus, I fully concede that I cannot make it through this life, much less this day, on my own. Remind me of my dependence on you. Lead me to seek your blessings and grace. Lead me to long for and enjoy your presence. Thank you for your love that knows no bounds.

WEDNESDAY

HEBREWS 13:20-21

Bronwyn Siebert

This past year, I became a mom of two children. When our son was born, I naively thought that since I had done this before just two short years ago, my transition would be easy. Navigating life with a newborn and toddler is proving exhausting, challenging, and sin revealing. It is incredibly difficult some nights to walk down the hall for the third time to nurse my son back to sleep, or to motivate a three-year-old to pick up her toys, or to find space to invest in my marriage when my energy is zapped by the end of the day. If I have ever needed the message of the gospel to permeate every corner of my life, it is now.

Hebrews 13:20-21 give us this closing benediction:

> *"Now may the God of peace who brought again from the dead our Lord Jesus, the great Shepherd of the sheep, by the blood of the eternal covenant, equip you with*

everything good that you may do his will, working in us
that which is pleasing in his sight, through Jesus Christ, to
whom be glory forever and ever. Amen."

Let this good Word sink into your soul. The God of peace, the great shepherd, equipping me to do his will, working out all things in me to make me more like Jesus, which is pleasing to the Lord. When I hear the crying baby over the monitor, God equips me to rise out of bed and care for him. When I want to tell my toddler, "I am not your servant!", God works the gospel into my heart and helps me joyfully bend down again to pick up the mess at the end of the day. When I would rather sleep than talk about things with my husband, the God of peace unites our hearts together.

What a wonderful savior. This season, may the hope we have knowing Christ Jesus was raised from the dead, equip us to do his work in our lives, giving all glory to him, because he alone can do it.

Lord, we thank you that in all seasons of life, the truth of your
gospel intervenes in our hearts. Thank you for the promise
we have in Hebrews 13. You truly deserve all the glory,
forever. Amen.

THURSDAY

2 THESSALONIANS 2:16-17

Justin Edgar

*Now may our Lord Jesus Christ himself, and God our Father,
who loved us and gave us eternal comfort and good hope
through grace, comfort your hearts and establish them in
every good work and word.*

The benediction of our Lord is meant to be a source of great
comfort to us. I love comfort. I'm an enneagram 7, which
means my deepest need is to avoid pain. To put it positively,
I love comfort. Comfort for me means no pain. Nothing too
hard. This means benediction is speaking my love language.

Here in 2 Thessalonians, Paul is helping this church to
face the reality of a man of lawlessness who will bring pain
upon the church. This agent of Satan has been unleashed
on God's bride. The lawless one will separate Jesus' people.

He will reveal who loves Jesus and who is just playing the game. That sounds both painful and scary. And yet the call is to stand firm. To not shrink back even in the face of such discomfort.

When I experience discomfort, I like to withdraw back into comfort. A nap perhaps, or a tv show in a man cave, or a good book, or time with some friends and my family who might help me forget it all. I'm not saying this is shrinking back, but it might be. Standing firm seems like a lot of standing, and I want to be treated like George Constanza's security guard — give me a cozy chair while I watch the door most likely asleep.

So how does Paul finish the call to stand firm? He gives the people the cozy chair in the good word of the Jesus blessing. He tells this waiting people that Jesus himself loves them and has implanted them into an alternative mode of time called eternal life, and that this hope is to be their comfort, the means by which they comfort themselves and are established in doing good in their words and their deeds.

Benediction is a means of grace. It is a God given way for us to be rehabituated and restoried. What is most true of you in the face of discomfort is the comfort of you being set outside of this time into eternity. You dwell secure even as the lawless man breathes his hot breath on your neck. Even as you feel the hot air of discouragement and loss. God is benedict-ing you! And this word is to be a means of your good words and work in the face of that hot breath.

God help us to receive your good word, and may it empower and embolden us to live secure in the face of pain, loss and the lawless man. Amen.

FRIDAY

JUDE 25-26

Justin Edgar

Now to him who is able to keep you from stumbling
and to present you blameless before the presence of
his glory with great joy, to the only God, our Savior, through
Jesus Christ our Lord, be glory, majesty, dominion, and
authority, before all time and now and forever. Amen.
~ Jude 25-26

Jude is one short book. This is good for quiet times. You get to Jude and are like one chapter, and you're done for the day. Feels good. Jude is a book however about contending for faith. This seems less awesome. I don't like a lot of conflict. How about you? In a few short words, Jude manages to contend for the faith by fighting back the false teachers and calling his church to persevere. And then he ends with a blessing upon them.

What does contending with false teachers and teaching

look like? Well, it looks like walking through the story of the Bible in some fascinating ways. If you never read Jude, you should check it out. You might have some questions. Jude doesn't pull any punches with these false ones. He says, they are grumblers, malcontents and loud-mouthed boasters.

But like Paul in Thessalonians, the call is similar. Stand firm. I am praying for you. Build yourself up. Keep yourself in the love. Wait for God's mercy, and then have mercy on the doubters who aren't yet where you are. When you have mercy, you are snatching them out of the fire. What an image? Have mercy on those who doubt, because of this false teaching...and when you do, you are a body snatching fireman. Boom!!

What things in your world, our age are perplexing to you about following Jesus? What things are tempting to you, that seem to fall outside of historic Christian faith? I'm guess you might be able to name a few. Maybe it is the doctrine of hell or modern day sexual ethics or maybe the finer points penal substitution. Jude doesn't pull punches with the teachers, and he doesn't stop throwing out fire-retardant mercy to those caught in their hot air. If you are caught in the hot air of these things, Jude is showering you with the drenching words of mercy.

Jude ends his letter dripping words of blessing. He says, there is One who will keep you from stumbling. There is One to present you blameless. There is One who brings great joy. Those are all things you need by the way as you doubt. You need another to hold you up, carry you along, take away the heat and fill you with joy...joy isn't absorbed by fire, it soaks it up instead. The one is Jesus, and this is why all glory, majesty, dominion and authority are his.

Jesus, we need you. We need you as we contend and fight for the faith. Contending can be a good thing. Help us not to be warrior children who are always picking fights, but help us to contend on essentials. Help us in our doubts too, as we are dizzy, caught up in the wash of the debates, give us mercy. Dose the flame of our doubts with the waves of Your mercy. Amen.

WEEKEND REFLECTION

MARCH 23 -24

CJ Green[1]

This year for Lent , I decided not to get crazy. In the past, especially as a kid, I'd sometimes give up three things at once, candy, my Gameboy, and fun in general. In the absence of those worldly distractions, I'd take up the terribly sanctified tendency of comparing and contrasting my virtue against my brother's: "Mom, he's playing Backyard Baseball, again..."

This year, none of that. I wanted to do something low-key. I wanted to spend a little time every morning praying. And not for any reason other than that, even now, that just sounds like a really nice way to start the day. But when I imagined prayer, in this context, I didn't just mean saying, "Hi God, it's me. Can you help?" and calling it a day. That seemed like a cop-out. I wanted to do something a little more poetic, something a little more meaningful—something like 10-15 minutes of quiet meditation, capped off with either some journaling or a dark cup of coffee. That's it. Just talking to God. Or to myself, about God. Either would have been fine. What I ended up doing was neither.

This year, on the first day of Lent, I woke up early. The sun had risen a little bit earlier than it had on the previous day, which is exactly what I had expected, having learned that 'Lent' is derived from some old Germanic word meaning 'the lengthening of the days.' A soft morning light pressed in through the window. I woke up, prayed, and did exactly what I had resolved to do, and felt great about it.

What happened after that is something of a blur. In the days that followed, I found myself busier than I'd expected. My schedule was in flux. Mornings came and went, with coffee but no prayer. I made one excuse, which turned into two. "I'll pray later today," I thought. And when "later today" came and went, I told myself I could miss one day. Grace, right? What's one day? What's two days? I stopped counting. I eventually forgot it was Lent. This past week, the time change put the nail in the coffin. Every minute of extra sleep I can get, I'm taking.

That first day of Lent seems so far away now, like from another life. The hope I had felt, that I could finally be the kind of person who takes time out of his day to really connect with the Lord on a regular basis...that hope has all but dissolved and given way to something more akin to a low-simmering anxiety. Yesterday I wondered if I could just restart, get a clean slate. How many more weeks until Easter? Is it too late to try again? The answer is, of course, I can get a clean slate. Of course it's never too late. But for what?

Often, when I think of Lent, I think, in the same moment, of the highly-anticipated Easter morning. I imagine going to church, the morning sun once again filtering in, this time through stained glass. I like to think of myself walking into the service having survived the desert season, here to party, ready to celebrate the resurrection. I like to think of myself as resurfacing, a new and better me—and on Easter, no less, which is, coincidentally, the time when Jesus, too, resurfaced, a new and better Him. On Easter, Jesus and I would celebrate our accomplishments together. I know of course that all of this misses the point.

You can learn a lot from Lent. You can learn a lot by abstaining from worldly things or committing to spiritual disciplines. For me, though, Lent has always yielded yet another pseudo-humorous reminder of my weakness. If you were to put me in the desert for forty days and the devil appeared and offered me bread, I now know for sure that I would take it. If he offered me my own kingdom...? Yes please.

This is a classic case of me misunderstanding my role in the scheme of things, because the reality is, I'm *not* going to the desert for forty days. Jesus already did that. He fasted for forty days so I don't have to. He died the brutal death, which I deserved, so that I don't have to. I am spared. "Where, O death, is your victory? Where, O death, is your sting?" Lent: add it to the list of things I can't do but Jesus can.

Obviously, I would still love a quiet morning of meditation and soft, pastel light. But for now, when I flip out of bed and groggily pour myself a cup of muddy joe and say, "Hi God, it's me. Can you help?"...for now, that isn't a cop-out. For now, that's more than enough.

WEEK FOUR

CALL TO WORSHIP

Justin Edgar

And the angel said to me, "Write this: Blessed are those
who are invited to the marriage supper of the Lamb."
And he said to me, "These are the true words of God."
Then I fell down at his feet to worship him, but he said to me,
"You must not do that! I am a fellow servant with you and
your brothers who hold to the testimony of Jesus. Worship
God." For the testimony of Jesus is the spirit of prophecy.
~ Revelation 19

"Worship God!" That's what the angel said to John on the island of Patmos, as he came to the end of the Revelation, and talked about heaven and the marriage supper of the lamb. Don't worship me! Worship God! Ok, angel. You just revealed to me the end of the grand story, I was slain in the

Spirit and fell down like a dead man, and then I was resusci-
tated. That was pretty powerful, can't I worship you or that?
No. Worship God!

Last week I watched the documentary *Free Solo*. It is about
the attempt by rock climb Alex Honnold to free solo climb
El Capitan in Yosemite National Park. It's an incredible
movie. And it's a great lesson about you are what you love. It
is a lesson in worship.

Alex worships perfection. It is what he is after. To rock
climb El Capitan with no ropes and the threat of his death
will require it. Perfection is a cruel taskmaster. But it
promises an encounter with the transcendent. Alex wants
the transcendent. He longs for it. Desires it. He just thinks
the only way to know it is through a mountain and a feat of
perfection. So, he goes to work. He practices and practices
the climb. He creates a written script of the movements. He
rehearses it. And then he embodies it and worships. The
mountain and perfection is his quest for transcendence. If
there is no threat of death, then there is no real cost, and
thus perfection isn't really required.

It reminds me of the Foster Wallace quote that I have
shared with you a few times:

> In the day-to-day trenches of adult life, there is no such
> thing as atheism. There is no such thing as not
> worshipping. Everybody worships. The only choice we
> get is what to worship. And an outstanding reason for
> choosing some sort of god or spiritual-type thing to

worship—be it JC or Allah, be it Yahweh or the Wiccan mother-goddess or the Four Noble Truths or some infrangible set of ethical principles—is that pretty much anything else you worship will eat you alive. If you worship money and things—if they are where you tap real meaning in life—then you will never have enough. Never feel you have enough. It's the truth. Worship your own body and beauty and sexual allure and you will always feel ugly, and when time and age start showing, you will die a million deaths before they finally plant you. On one level, we all know this stuff already—it's been codified as myths, proverbs, clichés, bromides, epigrams, parables: the skeleton of every great story. The trick is keeping the truth up front in daily consciousness. Worship power— you will feel weak and afraid, and you will need ever more power over others to keep the fear at bay. Worship your intellect, being seen as smart—you will end up feeling stupid, a fraud, always on the verge of being found out.

The insidious thing about these forms of worship is not that they're evil or sinful; it is that they are unconscious. They are default settings. They're the kind of worship you just gradually slip into, day after day, getting more and more selective about what you see and how you measure value without ever being fully aware that that's what you're doing.[1]

Alex slipped into this worship of perfection by learning its rhythms from his demanding parents and their detached emotions and rigid expectations. Perfection was the greatest ideal, and since everybody worships and since our Secular Age says this immanent frame is all there is, transcendence has to come from somewhere. So...perfection, a mountain, and no harness is as good as anything else.

As the film ends, Alex wants to cry, but can't. He can't even celebrate the unbelievable feat. He can't enter the moment fully. At some level, you can see how the most perfect day and perfect climb is fleeting, as he says some young kid watching this will do something even bigger or greater, shoot maybe even I will. The transcendence of the moment is so illusive, heaven remains untouched. And the reality of this is crushing.

John is called to get to his feet. There is only one that is worthy of our worship. There is only who object of worship that won't crush us. And the trick is what is conscious. John goes to his knees the minute there is a hint of the transcendent. It is what we do. We skim the surface and feel the rush and we fall down. Our default setting is worshipper, and we slip into it. But God still calls. God still calls. God still calls. Into our quests for perfections and are groping the immanent frame. God still calls. Worship me! And then he sends his messengers to tell us to get up, stop worshipping me or that or him or her ... Worship God!

MONDAY

PSALM 5:7-8

Daniela Byers

I'm in a season of asking God to deepen my walk with him and my dependence on him. I keep coming back to this idea of the Lord's steadfast love. As I've spent time trying to grasp the idea of a moment by moment communal relationship with the Lord, he continues to bring me back to this idea... that he's already here, already nearby, already listening, already leading, already making paths straight.

My question has been, how do I answer this call of God, this call to daily moment by moment worship? Daily life is loud (and so are the kids!) and busy, my job is challenging with too many never-ending tasks, and the house gets messy and so do my thoughts and relationships. How can I even hear His call with all the constant hubbub?

In the morning, I come. I sit. The lights are off. My hands are open. My eyes are closed, and I say, "Here I am Lord. Entering your house. Your Word says your love is steadfast. (Why can't I feel it sometimes? Are you even listening?) I want to follow well, Lord. I felt like such a failure yesterday. (Why does the dog eat everyone's socks? Do we have anything I can cook for dinner?)"

You see the problem, even in the midst of trying to answer the call to worship, is that the hubbub takes over! The distractions are many! And then more thoughts creep in. "This communing with God stuff is for the birds! I can't meditate! I can't even focus on God for more than 30 seconds straight!"

This scripture brings me rest. It's not through my own ability to concentrate, or to drown out the noise, or to check off the boxes, or to be somehow "good" at it walking with God—whatever that means. I answer His call to worship—I come to Him—THROUGH his abundant and steadfast love. His love is abundant—there's more of it available than I will ever need. His love is steadfast—it's truer, safer, stronger, and more steady than all my blunderings and shortcomings. When I remember these truths, it's much easier to hear and answer the call to worship.

Lord, create a desire in me to answer your call to a moment by moment dependence and trust. Only through your abundant and steadfast love do I enter your house. Give me ears eager to hear your voice, eyes able to see You working in the world, and feet quick to run to worship.

TUESDAY

PSALM 66:1-4

Justin Edgar

Come and see what God has done:
he is awesome in his deeds toward the children of man.
~ Psalm 66:1-4

We are all witnesses. I love that Nike ad for Lebron James.
It features Lebron, the King, and countless adoring
onlookers who are witnesses to his glory. The billboards
emblazoned with the Nike Swoosh and with the bold letters
—WITNESS.

Worship is witness.

We behold, and we become.

Worship is witness.

In Psalm 66, the psalmist calls God's people to respond
to what they have seen. To worship the awesome deeds of

God. Deeds like the exodus, where God delivered His people from their oppressors by parting the seas and causing them to walk on dry land. Or maybe he is pointing to the dividing of the rivers of the Jordan, so the people could pass on to the promised land.

Witness!

We don't just witness with our eyes. For the receivers of this psalm, they didn't see these acts. But they have rehearsed it. In ritual of Passover, they recount the power of their promise keeping God. They become witnesses by their ears and the rest of their bodies. They embody witnessing.

Just like the kids in the Lebron ad. They become Lebron on the court, re-enacting his every movement even down to the headband and the Nikes.

Witness.

God calls us to worship Him, embodying the story of His rescuing love, seeing, hearing, feeling, smelling, tasting.

Witnessing.

Worshipping.

God help me to be a witness to your great deeds, to come and see what you have done and then to embody that story in my story for the story of the world. Amen.

WEDNESDAY

PSALM 95

Stephen Siebert

Often when I am sitting in church, I find my mind wandering to other things. Why is it so hard for me to sit through church and focus on the worship of God? Why do we so easily forget what Jesus has done for us and what that means for our lives?

Psalm 95 is a call to worship God. The psalmist talks of praising the "rock of our salvation" and making joyful noises to our great king. God has done wonderful things in our lives, the greatest of course, rescuing us from our sins and granting us salvation. This alone is enough for us to jump for joy and praise the name of Jesus! But, along with this joy, there is a reverence in this Psalm. It says, "let us worship and bow down, let us kneel before the Lord", reminding us that in our worship we also must approach God with humility and respect. The final part of the Psalm is a warning for us to not harden our hearts, like the

Israelites did outside of the promised land, causing them to wander in the desert.

I read a scripture like this Psalm, understanding it in my mind, but it is much harder to understand it in my heart. I struggle with feeling the weight of my depravity, which in turn makes me ignorant of the grace that is given to me every day. This is why there is a call to worship at the beginning of church each week. It helps us remember who we are in light of God's love for us, causing us to praise his name with joy and humility.

Dear Jesus, help us to remember what you have done for us on the cross. Help us worship your name not only in church, but every day of our lives. Thank you for the grace that you give. Amen.

THURSDAY

PSALM 100

Justin Edgar

Make a joyful noise to the Lord, all the earth!
Serve the Lord with gladness!
Come into his presence with singing!
Know that the Lord, he is God!
It is he who made us, and we are his;
we are his people, and the sheep of his pasture.
Enter his gates with thanksgiving,
and his courts with praise!
Give thanks to him; bless his name!
For the Lord is good;
his steadfast love endures forever,
and his faithfulness to all generations.
~ Psalm 100

In Dead Poet's Society professor John Keating calls student Todd to sound a "Barbaric YAWP!" Todd is a sheepish kid, played beautifully by a young Ethan Hawke. Todd doesn't really know who he is. He is a bundle of nervous teenage energy. When "O' Captain, My Captian," played by Robin Willams, calls on Todd to do this, he is rehearsing the poet Walt Whitman and his sweat-toothed madman. He wants Todd to get in touch with his animal spirit.

You have an animal spirit. You are a liturgical animal—a desiring one. The Psalmist wants us to get in touch with that animal spirit, but not as some means of knowing ourselves necessarily, but as a means of knowing God and by extension ourselves. He calls out to us to make a "barbaric YAWP" to the Lord.

When was the last time you did that? What would it look like? I bet you are as sheepish as Todd. A little befuddled at such a call. You probably are looking around, making sure you are alone, there won't be any standing on chairs and raising your YAWP's. Maybe alone or maybe in the car, as long as there is no traffic.

The Dead Poet's Society motto is: *I went to the woods because I wanted to live deliberately. I wanted to live deep and suck out all the marrow of life. To put to rout all that was not life; and not, when I had come to die, discover that I had not lived.*

I want to live deliberately. I want to suck the marrow out of life. I want to rout out life and live. So I will raise by YAWP and live.

Friends, the Lord is good. His love is forever and it is loyal. And He made us to suck the marrow out of life. He made us to raise our "Barbaric Yawps." You are a liturgical animal made for Him. What would it look like for you to make a joyful noise unto the Lord.

Today is the day! Seize it. Make that joyful noise!

God, help us to respond to you in all sorts of ways. So fill our hearts and fan our affections that we might make our YAWPs to you! Amen.

FRIDAY

MATTHEW 11:28-29

David Breidenbach

The Greeks had a saying along these lines:

> *"It is difficult to find God and, when you have found him, it is impossible to tell anyone else about him."*

Jesus delivered his Matthew 11 message of invitation to people who were desperately trying to find God by frantically trying to do good, but were finding their tasks impossible and so they were driven to weariness and despair. It is an invitation to ALL people who are exhausted and worn-out from searching for truth and meaning in their lives because they were looking in all the wrong places!

It is Jesus' claim that the search for God and for meaning in our lives ends and begins in him:

> *"I am the way, and the truth, and the life. No one comes to the Father except through me."* John 14:6

And while this may sound like an unloving and completely self-serving claim to the exclusion of all other people's claims to a different path toward God, it is actually an invitation to stop the endless and frustrating searches for the things of God in the things of this world and to stop attempting to work out our own salvation. For they are not of God!

In Palestine, ox yokes were made of wood. The word translated "easy", as in "my yoke is easy" comes from the Greek word *"christos"* which can also mean *comfortable/well-fitting*. In other words, Jesus was saying "my yoke is well-fitting"- (which, along with a plowshare, is in the shape of a cross!).

Jesus was a carpenter. Oxen fitted to their yoke... Hmmm... that brings a bit of a different perspective! "My burden is well-fitted to your abilities (I already did the hard part, on the cross) and will serve you well... trust that I will lead you in paths that are straight and from which much fruit will be born."

Inspiration for a Christian comes, not from the fear of what God will do *to* you, but from the inspiration of what God—in Christ Jesus—has already done *for* you! This is something worth celebrating and is, indeed, our call to worship! For, you are a child of God for whom He has provided rest, comfort, and joy through the life, death, and resurrection of the Lord Jesus Christ! It is in this marvelous gift of God's grace in Christ alone, that we respond in worship with joy, praise, thanksgiving, and song to the glory of God!

Gracious and loving Father, the best gifts are those we have only to discover are already ours to receive. May this be our call to worship—knowing the sure and certain hope of a life everlasting in Christ Jesus—where our burdens, sorrows, and weeping are transformed into shouts of acclamation, worship, and praise! For, Yours is the glory. Amen!

WEEKEND REFLECTION

WHAT WOULD JESUS DO (FOR LENT)

Sarah Condon[1]

It is hard to believe that Ash Wednesday is upon us, with Lent coming in its wake. This season always stirs up some theological anxiety for me. I think it does for many of us. Each year, we hear the incredible story of Jesus heading into the desert. Hear from the Gospel of Luke:

> *Jesus, full of the Holy Spirit, returned from the Jordan and was led by the Spirit in the wilderness, where for forty days he was tempted by the devil.*

There is a widely preached theology which tells us that we can somehow identify with Jesus. This lens is all too often used to justify whatever behavior we are interested in spiritualizing. And so we get to be angry because Jesus turned over tables in the temple. We get to invoke righteous indignation at politicians or religious figures because Jesus yelled at the Pharisees and the hypocrites. At Lent, our WWJD theology is allowed to go into overdrive. We must "give up" something in order to identify ourselves with the suffering and self-denial of Jesus in the desert.

While all of this sounds earnest and well-intentioned, this theology misses the point–devastatingly so. Jesus wasn't just hanging out in the desert, dancing to the beat of a one man drum circle. Jesus was going toe to toe with the Satan himself. And there's nothing relatable about that for us.

The unhappy truth is that if we had been in the desert with the devil, and he had offered us the world as our kingdom we would have said: SURE, I'D LOVE TO RUN CAMELOT! THANKS FOR ASKING! WHERE'S MY CROWN?" Jesus has to face the devil down and deny him any and all authority because we are incapable of such sinlessness. And so, Lent is the time when the veil falls between who we think we could be and who Jesus must be for us.

People often talk of Lent as a journey, a pilgrimage, a sort of celestial road trip. We come by this assessment honestly. There are 40 days of Lent because Jesus spent 40 days in the desert. And so, the thinking goes, we must be on our own sort of ascetic journey, filled with self-denial and hard earned betterment. So we have Lenten lunches of soup and bread. We give up the modern trinity: chocolate, chardonnay, and Facebook. And then we blog about it.

Hear me clearly. I'm not saying that you shouldn't give up social media or vodka. I'm just suggesting you should go ahead and quit tomorrow in lieu of telling yourself that a Housewives of Atlanta moratorium is Lent-worthy. Because it is not. What Jesus did in the desert and what we attempt to do at Lent are almost wholly unrelated.

I would argue that Lent is not about us giving something up. In fact, it is not about our actions at all. Lent is a moment when we watch Jesus from afar. We are on the other side of the desert, watching him deny himself, bearing witness to his teachings and miracles, observing the disciples failing to stay awake, knowing that the agony of the cross is close at hand. Lent is not sad because we can't eat carbs. Lent is sad because we are forced to watch the slow, deliberate movement of our Savior from his ministry to his cross. And it reminds us of our sin and our powerlessness over it.

We were not in the desert for 40 days fending off the devil and all manner of temptation. Jesus was. For us. Because we are sinners. And as such, we would have taken all the devil offered.

Cue my Lenten jam:

Did we in our own strength confide, our striving would be losing;
Were not the right Man on our side, the Man of God's own choosing:
Dost ask who that may be? Christ Jesus, it is He;
Lord Sabaoth, His Name, from age to age the same,
And He must win the battle.
~ A Mighty Fortress is Our God, Martin Luther

WEEK FIVE

SINGING

Justin Edgar

"I sing because I'm happy."

What if I'm not happy? How can I sing?

Like what if I don't like musicals, and I'm not a foot-tapper. How can I sing?

I like talk radio and sports radio. I don't like any radio at all, how can I sing?

I don't sing in tune? This isn't my style of music? I have no rhythm? I'm pitchy. How can I sing?

I like hymns. I like choruses. I like Tomlin. Brian Whippo hates Tomlin. How can I sing?

Singing is part of every worship service I've ever attended. There is always multiples songs. Sometimes even a special. I had 7 songs at my wedding. 7 songs. None of them were congregational. So extra.

Why do we sing?

I love this quote by Reggie Kidd from his book *With One Voice:*

A theology that cannot be sung is not worth having.... Authentic Christian faith is not merely believed. Nor is it merely acted upon. It is sung - with utter joy sometimes, in uncontrollable tears sometimes, but it is sung.

We sing, because we have something to sing about. We sing cause we are liturgical animals. We sing because our faith is a practiced and embodied faith. The habit of singing is part of the acting. It is part of our "Barbaric YAWP." We sing because we are are lovers.

But maybe that just doesn't describe you...and so back to the first part — how do we sing? By singing. We sing by practicing singing. It may not be your first choice and then again, you may wish we could sing and not doing anything else. But the only way to sing, is to sing. Weird I know. But that is one of the things about spiritual practices and habits, about being a lover. Our hearts are aimed by our practices towards the end of — the Good Life. We are what we love. Singing makes us into lovers. We practice singing to love our God and know Him. We practice singing to be ONE with God's people, to wear our union with Christ. We don't sing because we are happy, but maybe we are a little bit happy because we sing.

MONDAY

PSALM 147

Emily Spare

Every night, at bedtime, my son requests to sing a song before we say goodnight. I recite the list of nursery rhymes he has become familiar with, "Twinkle Twinkle Little Star? Row, Row, Row Your Boat? Jesus Loves Me?" I continue listing song titles until I hear a decisive and emphatic, "YAH!" My husband and I stand over the bed singing silly lyrics about a teeny arachnid yet again pursuing an upward journey in a rain gutter.

Singing has been a part of my life since I was a similar age. It's likely that I became acquainted with my mom's voice while still in the womb as she participated in an adult choir at the time, and then grew up with music as an essential in our household. Piano was somewhat of a requirement in my education, and my middle school years pushed me into the first seats of the flute section in my school's band.

These silly songs I sing for my son are deeply ingrained

—they are the songs I sang with each instrument I was introduced to in order to bring a sense of comfort through nostalgia. And of course, vocal warm-ups used lyrical fragments from these melodies to emphasize breathing techniques or to help train the brain to hear a harmonious note. These tunes make up the foundation of my musical practice.

The Bible is full of God's people making music unto the Lord in all seasons of life. Psalm 147 is no different as it proclaims the praises of the Lord because of His very nature. And this psalm should be sung as the foundation of our musical practice of worship unto the Lord.

It is easy for me, after all of these years, to allow my husband to carry a deep base line for Old McDonald Had a Farm and sing dancing harmonies, exploring different musical keys for each animal sound our son interjects. But what about my melodies to my King? Is my practice to recognize the nature of my Lord and easily resound with grateful refrain stating the way He cares for His creation (take another look at Psalm 147:7-11).

Psalm 63:3 says, "Because your steadfast love is better than life, my lips will praise you." My practice of worship should become something so ingrained that my response to the nature of my God should be utter praise, unable to hold back at the chance to shout my God's great love to all that may hear.

Heavenly Father, remind me of the joy and privilege I have to sing unto You. Allow a response of song to become natural within me. Make me more like the psalmist, recognizing the praise you are due because of your nature: the Healer of broken hearts, the one who numbers the stars, the one who prepares rain for the earth, and makes grass grow on the hills. Amen.

TUESDAY

PSALM 98

Taeler Larsen

I grew up in a house full of music, singing and dancing. In fact, we basically lived in a real-life musical because we would *literally* break-out in joyous song as we responded to each other from across the house. Road trips were not about the destination. Road trips were for getting our family to join in harmony to the Wicked soundtrack all day long. My sister and I especially loved getting our dad to join in for the T-Swift playlists. In my family, music was often an emotive response to something (not always the right thing) that held our heart. We would sing in celebration and moments of joy and we would also sing in mourning and in confusion.

Psalm 98 tells of the Lord's work of salvation. In response to what He has done, all creation is called to join in joyous song to the one true God. The image of rejoicing that is given to us here is not of our typical, scheduled and safe time of "worship." This was not humans gathering in a building, sitting at least one chair apart from the individual next to them, quietly singing while staring straight ahead... this is loud, chaotic, and joyful worship. This is worship that is in response to God Himself. Here we see hearts aligned toward the One who deserves all the praise—the One who alone can satisfy. When was the last time that I not only *knew* that God was holy and good, but I *sensed* and *experienced* it? When was the last time that I encountered or remembered God and it caused me to fall to my knees in worship of Him?

God, take back my heart from the many things I cling to that fall short because they aren't You. When I see the marvelous things that you have done, let my heart be ready to praise you. Let me sing with all heaven and nature of the wonders of your love. Joy to the world!

WEDNESDAY

EPHESIANS 5:15-21

Emily Leslie

"Dissociation: The Great Escape... Dissociation is a psychological term used to describe disconnecting from full engagement with your body and the relationships around you. Dissociation is likely something you have been doing since childhood. Think about the hours of TV, video games, and Internet you consumed growing up. For many individuals, the distractions of technology were more consistent than a deep, loving engagement with meaningful relationships. We experience these dissociative moments every day and in almost any context."

Unwanted, Jay Stringer

The call in Ephesians 5 sounds to me like the practical response to this psychological term... look carefully, pay attention, pursue wisdom, don't get distracted by things that can lead you down a path of disconnection... promote what is true, remind yourself of it by any means possible, tell your friends, talk about it, sing about it, recount it in your heart, and make sure to dwell in gratitude on the present realities of your life, because they are a reminder of God's goodness.... That's my own paraphrase, but if you check out the Message version of this passage, it's not far off.

Dissociation is a great escape. It allows us to check out, ignoring the reality of our failures: lack of motivation, guilt, feelings of being overwhelmed, and anxiety... of course we want to flee reality. But it provides us only with an empty promise of relief, leaving us searching for the same escape day after day, in all varieties distraction. Jay Stringer goes on to share that "dissociation gives us an opportunity for what Jesus refers to as metanoia, translated as repentance. The better definition would be a turning or revolution (meta-) in the mind or consciousness (nous)." Then he points to another of Paul's arguments in this direction from Romans 12:2, to *be transformed by the renewing of your mind.*

Today, for me, turning my consciousness requires putting my phone down. To go sit on the back porch in silence. To turn the TV off. To observe and even participate in the sharp reality of disappointment that I would rather stifle, so that I may more fully experience the blessing and joy of my Savior Jesus Christ.

Father, you've called us to pay attention for our good, and your glory. Help me to trust that the relief I desire is not found in temporary distractions, but in the truth of your power, presence, and peace. Bring it to the front of my mind that the moments I've been given are worth boldly engaging in. Amen.

THURSDAY

ZEPHANIAH 3:14-20

Joshua Spare

Have you ever watched a movie or read a book where, as the plot is reaching the denouement, you get so caught up that you want to literally stand up and cheer? I certainly recall that elation from the first time of reading The Lord of the Rings: The Return of the King. All the Knights of Gondor and Riders of Rohan and all the forces of good have gathered at the Black Gate of Mordor in a final effort to throw their pitiful strength against the full might of the Dark Lord; Aragorn and Gandalf and Legolas and Gimli stand to give their all in an attempt to draw the eye of Sauron to them in the small hope that Frodo and Sam are yet alive and yet journeying toward the heart of Mount Doom to cast in the ring of power. The gallant little hobbit, Pippin, is standing amongst these tall men, struggling to keep back the forces of evil, and all seems lost:

"'So ends as I guessed it would,' his thought said, even as

it fluttered way; and it laughed a little within him ere it fled, almost gay it seemed to be casting off at last all doubt and care and fear. And then even as it winged away into forget-fulness it heard voices, and they seemed to be crying in some forgotten world far above:

'The Eagles are coming! The Eagles are coming!'"

What a joyful and exuberant chorus as the harbingers of salvation arrive! And, as merely a witness to this scene, I wanted to stand and shout! To rejoice that salvation had come!

Here at the end of prophecy of Zephaniah, after the proclamation of the coming of the wrath of the Lord against Judah, the Philistines, Moab, Ammon, Cush, Assyria, and Jerusalem, we turn to the hopeful anticipation of the Day of Lord, and Zephaniah commends, "Sing aloud, O daughter of Zion; shout, O Israel! Rejoice and exult with all your heart, O daughter of Jerusalem!" How easy it is to look upon the justice of God's wrath with fear and trembling; but how infrequently do I look to God's blessing and shout with praise and song?! Just as I am so drawn into Tolkien's story that I feel a desire to shout for joy, so too (and much more!) should I be immersed in the blessed story of redemp-tion that I am compelled to stand and shout and praise our great and just God! The excitement with which I remember "The Eagles are coming!" can perhaps be superseded as I remember "Christ *has* died! Christ *is* risen! Christ *will* come again!"

Praise You, God, for You have taken away the judgments against me! Help me to be filled with joy as I look to the day of your coming!"

FRIDAY

HEBREWS 2:12 & 13:15

Justin Edgar

I will tell of your name to my brothers and sisters; in the
midst your congregation I will sing your praise.
~ Hebrews 2

My voice has had some problems recently. Namely, its
gotten a little ragged and weak, which has caused me to not
have the upper registry range I had previously. It has lasted
a month or so. Sunday I was almost fully back, and then I
sung the Doxology. Maybe it isn't all the way back. I went
for the high note, and just couldn't get there, so I had to
drop it down a notch. In doing so I was reminded that
singing is not an individual thing. It is corporate. We sing
together, and dropping down an octave made me hear
everyone else even more clearly.

Together we sing one song. There might be different parts—melody and harmony, but it is one song. Here the preacher in Hebrews actually quotes Psalm 22. This song is a song of praise that points forward to the resurrected Messiah with suffering complete joining the congregation of heaven of all the redeemed in heaven. And here He calls His brothers and sisters to join Him in singing. They are all children of the Father, singing with one voice the praise of the Creator, the founder of their salvation, the one who makes all things good and holy. We sing our songs with Jesus. He is our brother worship leader leading us in singing.

This reminds me of two things in the writing Tolkien and Lewis. The first image comes from the first book in Chronicles of Narnia, The Magician's Nephew. This is the breathtaking scene:

> In the darkness something was happening at last. A voice had begun to sing.... It seemed to come from all directions at once.... Its lower notes were deep enough to be the voice of the earth herself. There were no words. There was hardly even a tune. But it was beyond comparison, the most beautiful noise he had ever heard. It was so beautiful Digory could hardly bear it.

After this scene those present looked above them and saw the blackness filled with stars, and each of them were singing as well. But the voice of the stars grew fainter as the voice of the one singing drew near. Wind came rushing, the blackness of the sky turned to grey, hills began to stand up around them, the sky changed to pink and then to a brilliant gold, and as soon as the voice swelled to the mightiest sound it could produce the sun rose over the hills. And from the sun's light they all could see the source of the singing, a large, golden lion standing in the middle of the valley. At this moment we read that two distinct reactions occurred from seeing the lion. Some of the party present there loved this singing so much they could remain before it for an eternity listening to its pleasure. Others present, the Witch and Uncle Andrew, could barely stand to be before it, and seemed as if all they wanted to do is run and hide in a hole in the ground to get away from it. The song began to change after this and the lion began walking toward the party standing there. With each step the singing lion took with its large paws trees and mountains and animals and rivers and flowers and all sorts of lovely things were bursting forth into existence, until finally, all was created. Narnia had been created by the voice of the lion. Aslan stood in the center of a circle created by the all the animals he had just made, and he said to them, "Narnia, Narnia, Narnia, awake. Love. Think. Speak. Be walking trees. Be talking beasts. Be divine waters."[1] The creating song of love sung by Jesus in the midst of the created congregation.

The second is Tom Bombadil—Tom is a mysterious character who lives deep in the woods. He is thought to be the oldest being in Middle-earth. And what does Old Man Tom do? He sings. He sings in rhythm and meter. He first appears when Merry and Pippin are trapped by Old Man Willow. When Frodo and Sam cry for out help, Tom appears and rescues them by singing. He is an emancipator. He is a freedom rider. He is unfazed by the power of the ring. He walks the forest singing his songs, and the woods obey him. Tom leads these pilgrims through the dangers of the night and forest, and he does it by singing. Tom is the redeemer-singer.

Here the author of Hebrews says the same of Jesus. Jesus creates us and redeems us and invites us to sing praise to God with Him. He is the singing one, and united to Him we become a singing people, singing the one song to the King.

Jesus, lead us in your song of creation and redemption. Help us to sing your one song together in the midst of your congregation both created and redeemed. Amen.

WEEKEND REFLECTION

Reggie Kidd[1]

I, too, am captivated by the vision of Christ now leading worship in the church, fulfilling the promise of Psalm 22:22: *"I will declare Your name to my brothers in the midst of the assembly I will sing a hymn to you"* (Hebrews 2:12). Maybe it is simply because I know how hard it is for certain kinds of people to consider singing alongside certain other kinds of people, but I am especially taken with the fact that it is specifically "in the assembly" that the Psalmist locates the Savior's singing.

What Songs does Jesus Sing?

Thoughts from Psalm 22:

- Jesus sings the Hebrew songs of covenant Faithfulness. (vs.23)

- Jesus sings the folk idioms from "all the families of the earth" (v.27)
- Jesus sings with the voice of the refined, the illuminati, the cultured. (v.29a)
- Jesus sings with all the grit and earthiness, with all the directness and rhythms of the "working poor." (v.26)
- Jesus sings among the saints who have gone before. (v.29b , Heb. 12:23)
- Jesus sings among the yet-to-be-born.(vv.30-31)

It's About His Song, Not Ours

When seen in the light of the person of Jesus, the church's Lead Worshiper, our squabbles over how to do it right—which group's aesthetic will be honored, and which group's dishonored—take on their true measure: they are pathetically small-minded.

While we try to pare His song down to a manageable repertoire, He is expanding it. While we are doing market research to decide whom we want to reach and, therefore, to whose aesthetic tastes we want to pander, the Singing Savior is distributing His magnificent voice across an increasingly wide spectrum of musical idioms. While we are dividing congregations along age lines, He is blending the songs of generations and nations and families and tribes and tongues to make sweet harmony, precisely through the differences, to the Father.

The day has come for us to mute our provincial songs, and start listening for His voice, for it is "like the sound of many waters" (Rev. 1:15), as rich and complex as the constitution of His people.

Jesus' voice is what counts, not ours. And His is the voice of the Jew and the Gentile, the poor and the rich, those who have already had their say and those who have not yet even come into being. There is a unity and diversity in the voices of His assembly which we may not be able to hold together on our own, but which the Risen Christ, because He is literally and vibrantly present among us, can.

WEEK SIX

CONFESSION OF SIN AND ASSURANCE OF PARDON

Justin Edgar

Have you ever walked into the middle of a move? Like you are flipping channels and land on a movie, but it has already started. I remember catching *Sleepless* staring Jaime Foxx this way. We were in Cabo, and one of the channels that I would flip through between siesta in my room was HBO-Latino. Sleepless was in English with Spanish subtitles. I flipped and started watching. And then I tried to play catch up. In fact, I watched a solid hour or so in the middle, and then we had to go to dinner. So I missed the end and the beginning. It was so frustrating. Later in the week, I finally caught the beginning, and things started to clear up, but I never got the end. I still haven't. I don't know how *Sleepless* ends. I should probably watch it.

Sometimes the confession of sin in our worship is framed this way. We come into worship, and as we enter confession, we think the story of confession is about the confessing. Like, I am a sinner. I know this clearly. And so I need to confess. However, that leading edge of sin and sinners, sometimes catches us like a blunt force instrument upon our oversized chins. It hits with a thud. Knocks us out cold. And then other times the story of confessing misses the mark entirely, as we just get tired of the sinner song. Yes, I'm a sinner, ugh I know. But this view of confessing is like catching the movie in the middle. We lose context.

The context of confession is vital. Confession is made by a people who have been called in, gathered by God to worship. It is a response to our promise-keeping God. He leads and we respond. He calls and we respond. He shows us our sin and we respond. Now that we've caught the beginning, let's not miss the end. Confession also comes with this kind of built in confidence, this anticipation of assurance. We have been promised that if we confess our sins, then he is faithful and just to forgive us our sins and cleanse us from all unrighteousness. This is the context of our confession.[1]

This context shapes us to be a people who are free to confess, because we have a God who reveals our need of confession. This word is a hard word. It is mirror and a tutor. It shows us who we are, and leads us to our deepest need, not behavior modification, but grace. We are a responding people. God is an initiating lover. The last word is a sure word. It is a word that frees us to confess. The first word says we need confession and the last word says we can confess. The law and the promise give us the context for confession. So, let us practice confession, and may it form us into a contrite and needy people. A people who sit on the edge of our seat, awaiting the end—the promise that to all those who repent and trust in Jesus—"Your sins are forgiven."

MONDAY

1 JOHN 1:5-9

Daniel Gettemy

It was pretty rare for me to get into much trouble as a child. Not that I didn't do things that I shouldn't; I broke the rules plenty of times! But I always had a hard time lying about it. If my mom suspected that I'd done something wrong, all she had to do was confront me about it and I would inevitably break down crying and confess. Sometimes she could just look at me and I'd lose it!

In our family confession always prompted mercy. If I confessed what I'd done, then mom was usually much more lenient on the punishment. If I lied about it or tried to cover up what I'd done—or blamed one of my other siblings—then mercy would give way to judgment. Sometimes it took my mom a few days to sort things out. Those were long days! It was like I was walking in the dark, all while pretending I was in the light.

But the gospel provides a different motive for confession. You see, it's the mercy of God that prompts us to confess our sin. It's because God has already punished our sin in Jesus, through His death on the cross, that we're motivated to confess our failings. We don't have to fear God's judgment; in Christ not only has our sin been judged, but we've been declared righteous as well! Not only were we crucified with Christ, but we've been raised with Him in justification!

That's why I love that our time of confession is at the front end of our worship service. So often I come to worship fully aware of my sin and failings throughout the week. But our time of confession brings the truth of the gospel—and the glory of God's mercy—back into full view. In the grace of God, I am, *we* are, already forgiven because of the cross of Jesus Christ. His mercy begs our confession and provides our forgiveness. We can go on in worship with a clean conscience and a pure heart.

Lord, thank you for your great mercy! Help me to live out my relationship with you with short accounts. May I never try to hide what You already know. May I never be afraid to confess what You've already provided forgiveness for. Amen.

TUESDAY

PSALM 51

Chelsea Warren

Lately, my life has consisted of a lot of spit up and dirty diapers. Not all will be able to relate specifically to this, but I am sure most have found themselves in a situation where there is constant mess and clean up. The routine for me usually goes like this: feed the baby, baby spits up on her clothes, I change her clothes, baby needs her diaper changed, I change her diaper, baby spits up on her clothes again. This happens at least 3-4 times a day. Most days it can be comical, but usually it is just annoying.

In Psalm 51, we are encountered with an immense amount of cleaning up that needs to be done. David, the writer of this psalm, realizes his filthiness—his sin. His sin has caused a huge mess consisting of adultery and murder—things that cannot just be swept up or wiped away. David repeats phrases like "wash me" and "cleanse me" in the psalm, showing us that his sin makes him unclean; he feels unclean. David knows that he has hurt others, but his sin is ultimately against God. *"Against you, you only have I sinned and done what is evil in your sight, so that you may be justified in your words and blameless in your judgment."* David deserves punishment, but instead he asks for mercy, begging God to make him right in His presence. *"Hide your face from my sins and blot out all my iniquities. Create in me a clean heart, O God, and renew a right spirit within me."*

Aren't we all like David in one way or another? Our sin creates messes just like his sin did—messy relationships, messy lifestyles, messy ways of handling conflict, etc. While God is going to clean up our messes one way or another, He still freely offers Himself to us to be made clean. David cried out to God and believed that God would answer. We too believe that, despite our sin, we can come to God in repentance and be made clean. The only way this can happen is through Christ. And ironically enough, Jesus washes us in such a messy and terrible way—death on a cross and the shedding of His Blood. God uses messes for His glory, never ours.

In the midst of changing diapers and cleaning spit up, I am reminded of how God must feel cleaning up our messes. Maybe sometimes He finds it funny, but most likely He gets frustrated, wondering why did we ever think "xyz" would be such a good idea. And still, He picks us up afterwards, just like I pick up my daughter, and carries us through life. He doesn't give up on us, He doesn't say that we are too dirty to receive love. He hears our cries, sees our suffering, and opens His arms.

Father, I realize that my sin causes messes that I cannot clean up on my own. Because of these messes, I am unclean. Forgive me for hurting those around me, for letting my messes affect others. Forgive me for ultimately hurting You.

May I remember, though, that my messes do not define me – that there is always an opportunity for redemption found in You. Thank you for Your unfailing love and carrying me through life, even when it is messy. Amen.

*On another note, if you need good music, the Modern Post (lead singer is the lead singer of Thrice) has a song all about Psalm 51 called White As Snow!

WEDNESDAY

LUKE 18:9-14

Justin Edgar

Meanwhile the tax man, slumped in the shadows,
his face in his hands, not daring to look up, said,
'God, give mercy. Forgive me, a (the) sinner.
~ Luke 18 (The Message)

Have you ever played the comparison game?

It's a game I play. I compare myself to other preachers for instance. I go to a conference and hear a guy, and think, hmm, I'm as good as that guy or I hear Tim Keller, and go, man I wish I was that guy. Maybe you do it with the way you look? Or how smart or not smart you feel? Or how good you are or not at your job. Or maybe there is a sibling who garners your envy, or maybe you are the one others are envious. You are out on the trail or scaling a rock wall with friends—who's better? We are good at this game.

Jesus hits on this in his parable about the two men who go to the temple to pray and confess. Both compare. One man, the religious one, compares himself to the sinner in the assembly with him. He thanks God that he is not like that man. This temptation is very real. We have a tendency to build circles and fences and walls. We like boundary marking, identity clarifying labels. He's the sinner. And I'm glad I'm not the sinner. My sister is such a mess up. My neighbor is such a liberal. My co-worker is such a Trump guy. I bet he owns a MAGA hat. My dad is so nosey. I can't believe the coach lets her start over my daughter. Labels, boundaries, who's in and who's out. I do it, and I bet you do too. Jesus says, we religious people are pretty good at it.

Now the other man in the parable compares himself too. He is slumped in the shadows, avoiding eyes and questions. He can't bare to look at the assembly or up toward God. This man is the tax man. He is a known extortioner. He is a trader of his own people. He is a despised man, and if people know him, then they know this is his rep. But this is also why he is there. He is longing for absolution to his very real problem, hopeful that this time it might hit, this time, he might know forgiveness. So slumped in the shadows, he prays his comparison prayer. God, have mercy on me THE sinner. He throws himself in with the lot, but he knows he has no righteousness to throw around. He just has his sin. He just has his guilt. He just has his shame. So he throws it out there—comparing himself with a world of sinners and using the definite article, says, forgive me— THE sinner. Our bibles use - a, but it is - the. He is worse than not just some or most, but all. The comparison game has left him undone—there is none righteous no not one. He is not. He is the worst.

Jesus then comments: This tax man, not the other, went home made right with God. If you walk around with your nose in the air, you're going to end up flat on your face, but if you're content to be simply yourself, you will become more than yourself.

God, help us to be ourselves, not more than ourselves. Help us not to posture or primp. Help us not to throw our right-eousness around. Help us to see we need to confess not only our bad things, but our good things as well. Our unrighteous-ness and our self-righteousness. And have mercy, O' Lord, have mercy, for I am THE sinner. But you are THE savior. Amen.

THURSDAY

Rachel Whippo

The first step to getting over an addiction is acknowledging you have one in the first place. As human beings, we are inherently addicted to sin. In fact, it is so deeply rooted in us that it is impossible to think of ourselves without sin, "holy and blameless" like Christ. But that is what the Gospel promises. Through Christ we are freed from our sin, but how? Well, like with any addiction, we must first acknowledge it. Through prayer and confession, we are freed from sin through the healing blood of Christ.

Sin, and the guilt that comes with it, can become physically and mentally painful and draining. I am someone who hates the feeling of keeping secrets because it takes a physical toll on me and causes anxiety and stress. Sin is the same. It slowly eats away at you through guilt, and until it is released, the toll it takes on your mind and body can feel unbearable. But thankfully as Christians we are promised a relief through confession and prayer. Because God promises that through acknowledgement of our sin, he will take away the guilt of our sin and surround us with his faithful love.

This is why it is so important to have a confession of sin on Sunday mornings. I often get to that part of the service on Sundays and realize I haven't thought about, acknowledged or confessed my sin at any other point in the week, and because of that I have been carrying the burden of guilt with me consciously or unconsciously. It is important not just for our spiritual health, but for our physical and mental health to acknowledge and confess the sin in our lives and ask God to take the burden of our sin from us because it is too heavy to carry on our own.

Heavenly Father, please help us throughout the week to acknowledge our sin and confess it to you. Let us rest in the knowledge that through your Son the guilt of our sin is washed away. Help us through each confession to become more like you. In your name, we pray. Amen.

FRIDAY

JOHN 21:15-19

Joanna Hinks

I've got a confession to make. The weekly confession of sin at church is the part of the service I both love and hate. It's those two or three sins—you may have your own—that I find myself confessing week after week after week. There's even a name for it: "besetting sin." So I come to the time of confession squirming inside because once again I haven't learned.

The internal conversation goes something like this:

Jesus: "Joanna, do you love me?"
Me: "Of course I love you, Jesus!"
Jesus: "Do you love me more than *that* sin?"
Me: "Oh. That."

There's a reason we use the symbol of the rooster. Like Peter, we are betrayers by nature, going back to the same old sins no matter how vehemently we've declared our allegiance just last Sunday. One of the lessons of this passage is that in Jesus, God's forgiveness is patient and persistent. Every week, he gives us another chance to answer the question: "Do you love me?" As uncomfortable as that question may be, Jesus loves *us* enough that he doesn't allow us to continue cheerfully singing his praises one moment and breaking God's law the next.

And that's why I also love the time of confession. Because when I confess my sin, God doesn't reject my confession as worthless currency (even if I find myself wondering why He doesn't). The truth is, any time I try to make changes by my own strength, it is worthless. So confession brings me to the point of recognizing how helpless I am to stop sinning, and thrusting myself on God's mercy again. Week after week after week.

Jesus, once again I come before you and confess that I don't love you as much as I should. I want to stop sinning, but I'm powerless to make lasting changes in my life by my own efforts. Break through my stubbornness with your mercy and kindness. Give me a new life by living in me with your righteousness.

WEEKEND

PALM SUNDAY

Andrew Peterson[1]

"Hosanna!" We cried, and we waved our palms,
Standing outside the church on Palm Sunday.
We sang songs of praise, read lessons and Psalms,
And then came the Gospel reading. The way
It usually happens, the celebrant
Follows the cross and Bible down the aisle,
And we all turn to face them. The moment
Reminds us of the Incarnation while
The scripture is read. God did become flesh.
He dwelt among us. But it's Holy Week,
And things change so that we feel it all fresh,
The arrest, trial, crucifixion: we shriek,
"Crucify him! Crucify him! Release
Barabbas!" How quickly hosannas cease.

WEEK SEVEN

PASSING THE PEACE

Justin Edgar

There is a rhythm to the words—"may the peace of the Lord be always with you... and also with you." Pronouncement—response—pronouncement. Greg Thompson, a pastor, shared a story about his son when he went to apologize to his sister. Their pattern became pronouncing this word of peace. The boy apologizes and the sister says, "that's ok." And then she says to her brother—"may the peace of Christ be with you," and then the little brother says, "and also with you." It's sweet. But it's also real.

Reconciliation is one of the marks of the church. It is something we need to practice, and something we need help to do. We aren't very good at passing peace, at practicing reconciliation. It is so much easier to bury the hatchet by NOT. SAYING. A. THING. That's a preferable mode of reconciliation for us. But the problem is—it's not reconciliation. It is just conflict-avoidance. And it's easier, or so we think. But then because it a thing, and it isn't resolved, it becomes an actual thing. A thing that holds power over you, as you have become resentful, embittered and distant. You didn't want to say anything, so you can't in the end, end up saying anything. You just withdraw from relationship or you just fake it. And that isn't a way for us to live.

The other preferable response to a lack of peace is to gossip our way around peace. We just talk about what that person did or didn't do with a few of our closest friends. So instead of passing the peace, we create chaos through "the pornography of the mouth." That's what pastor Scott Saul's calls gossip. It is essentially taking a person and dressing them down and objectifying them for our own satisfaction. It's a cheap thrill that offers zero commitment to the person being objectified. Zero-commitment. It is much easier to talk about a person than talk to the person. So, instead of passing the peace and practicing reconciliation, practicing peace and sharing our offenses, we objectify and get off on what wrong or perceived wrong has been done to us by them. And it is exhilarating.

Passing the peace is meant to be a formational practice of peace-making and peace seeking, because of our peace giving savior Jesus. We are a people who have peace, because Jesus has conquered the powers of sin and death by His own body. His body is our peace offering. And by it we can be healed, reconciled, re-united. "So, the peace of Christ be always with you — and also with you."

MONDAY

JOHN 14:15-31

Justin Edgar

Peace I leave with you; my peace I give to you.
Not as the world gives do I give to you.
Let not your hearts be troubled, neither let them be afraid.
~ John 14:15-31

When people move away from Albuquerque, my heart gets troubled. I start to worry about the viability of our church. I think about how much that person gives or does or how their bum in the seat means a lot to a church trying to grow to have more bums in seats. Or how their story, their transformation impacts other stories and other transformations. For me, it is a peace robber.

The disciples are being told how Jesus is about to leave.

Now, no offense, but like you guys aren't Jesus. So, I imagine the disciples are quite troubled about news of Jesus departure. He's kinda a big deal. Jesus knows their frame, and so he reassures them, that his going is actually a good word, because of the Helper. The Helper will teach you and make you remember all the things I've said to you. The Helper will bring you peace. This word peace isn't just like internal peace or relational peace, but it is shalom. Wholistic peace—peace of body, mind, spirit, emotions. I am not just healing conflict here, like the world. I'm not just giving "peace a chance." I'm not just bring world peace. By sending my Spirit, I am sending you my shalom.

And then he breaks it down even further. He says, so don't be troubled by my departure. Don't be afraid by all this talk of my death. He frames the coming of the Spirit and the shalom the Spirt is bringing with His kingdom and eternity. He says I am going away and if I go away that means I am reigning as a king with the Father, and this means that the ruler of this age isn't the king any more, not that he ever was really. But He will have no claim to the throne. And the Spirit is my emissary, sent to be with you so that the world will know that I am the Father's and the Father is mine.

The peace that Jesus gives us is a peace secured by Jesus death, resurrection and ascension. It is peace that dwells with us by God's spirit. Because Jesus is reigning in heaven, this means the Spirit of the prince of peace has taken up residence not just in the world, but inside of us. And he will bring his wholeness not just to us, but through us to the world. So, let's roll. Let's do this, Jesus says. You have my peace, now, make us instruments of your peace.

Jesus, thank you for your Spirit, who brings us Your peace.

May He make us a peace filled people, passing that peace to all we meet. May we in this world of trouble and devils, not be afraid, for you are with us. Amen.

TUESDAY

MATTHEW 5:9

Emily Leslie

Maybe I'm a two... I've always related with the role of "people pleaser"... maybe a six... My mom is a six, and we're practically the same person... or a one... I've known crippling perfectionism... as I read through the descriptions of the Enneagram Personality Types for the first time I felt really, really lost. Identity-less. I could be any of these... Until I got to the nine...

> "We have sometimes called the Nine the crown of the Enneagram because it is at the top of the symbol and because it seems to include the whole of it. Nines can have the strength of Eights, the sense of fun and adventure of Sevens, the dutifulness of Sixes, the intellectualism of Fives, the creativity of Fours, the attractiveness of Threes, the generosity of Twos, and the idealism of Ones. However, what they generally do not

have is a sense of really inhabiting themselves—a strong sense of their own identity. Ironically, therefore, the only type the Nine is not like is the Nine itself. Being a separate self, an individual who must assert herself against others, is terrifying to Nines."

THE WISDOM OF THE ENNEAGRAM, P.
316-317

Bleh. At first I liked the sound of a personality type named "Peacemaker"... Jesus' words from the Sermon on the Mount came to mind... Great! My personality type is blessed! But reading the description of the nine, it becomes easily apparent that the peace that Jesus is referring to, is not the same as the peace described in this earthly personality construct (see John 14:27... should have known). And the peace that I long for as a "Peacemaker" is still very much in need of the transformative work of the Holy Spirit for me to be called a "son of God".

God Himself is a peacemaker, and through the narrative of redemption he authors, enacts, and invites us into this ministry of reconciliation (2 Corinthians 5:17-21). God makes a sacrifice for harmony, and then invites us to do the same... and informs us that there will be struggle, trial, and suffering along the way (Genesis 3:14-19, John 16:33, James 1:12). As a nine, my temptation is to retreat from anything that threatens my tranquility. I value internal and external peace so highly, that I will idolize it, anxiously chase after it (ironic), and neglect to address the dark clouds of hardship altogether. But being a peacemaker as a child of God gives me a deeper identity and a higher call. I can step into tension, trusting that God has already established harmony, and that the purpose of my identity as a representation of God's peace is much deeper than my momentary experience of peace.

Father, help me to love what You love. Comfort my desperation for temporary peace, with Your peace that surpasses all understanding. May I be released from the burden of maintaining earthly peace to protect my inner stability, and strengthened in boldness to promote peace that is everlasting. Amen.

WEDNESDAY

COLOSSIANS 3:15

Daniel Gettemy

Several years ago, I travelled to an area of South Sudan that was just south of the war-torn Darfur region. It was a bleak place. The scattered people of that area lived with the constant tension of the potential for war, coupled with the ongoing struggle with famine and disease. Theirs was a hard life. Often, it was a fearful life.

But when Sunday came, something wonderful would happen. There was an itinerant pastor that would show up on Sundays. There wasn't necessarily a set time for his arrival because often he would be walking in from another village many, many miles away. He was a former "lost boy" of Sudan who'd come back to bring the gospel to his warring nation. And when this pastor would show up, all the Christians in the area would know it was time to gather for a worship service. These were people who once were Muslim or Animist, but who had heard the gospel and come to faith in Jesus Christ.

Not everyone in the area was Christian. As a matter of fact, most weren't. But what a beautiful thing it was when those who were Christians gathered to worship the Lord together! It was like a Peace Summit was taking place in an embattled area!

They didn't have a building. Instead, they met under the shade of a large tree on the outskirts of the village. There was no sound system. But when they sang – oh, how their praises filled the air! They had no Bibles of their own. And yet they hung upon every word that their pastor proclaimed from the Scriptures. There was a peace that was palatable in their midst. It was Jesus Christ, through His gospel, that produced that peace in their midst. And it was His peace that they were diligent to offer to one another, as well as to share with anyone who would venture into their gathering.

The apostle Paul exhorts us to *"let the peace of Christ rule in your hearts, to which indeed you were called in one body."* To "rule" means to be the arbitrator. Indeed, we've been called from many places and many backgrounds into one body; and it is the peace that Christ has given us through His cross—peace with God and peace with one another—that is to be the arbitrator of our hearts.

And while we may not live in a war-torn country, we must still be intentional about what it is that will rule our hearts and our relationships with one another. Which is why, when we take a moment to "pass the peace" in our worship service, it's more than just saying "Hello" to one another. It is a response of grace; an extension of forgiveness and fellowship to all who gather with us in the name of Christ. And it is this peace, displayed in thankfulness and joy, that sets the Church apart wherever it gathers in the world.

Jesus, thank you for giving us Your perfect and abiding peace. Please help me to let the peace that you've given be the arbitrator of the relationships in my life. Help me to forgive, even as I've been forgiven. Help me to share my life with others, even as You share the Triune fellowship of Father, Son, and Holy Spirit with me. Amen.

THURSDAY

A MAUNDY THURSDAY REFLECTION OF PEACE

David Zahl[1]

Francois Clemmons played the role of friendly Officer Clemmons on Mister Roger's Neighborhood for over 25 years. It turns out that Clemmons was the first black actor to have a recurring role on a children's television series. I had no idea. But what makes this so poetic is that Mr Rogers had him play a policeman, AKA a representative of law (enforcement). It was not an easy thing for Clemmons to do, given how police officers were viewed in *his* own neighborhood, i.e., as arbiters of oppression and cruelty. Rogers was clearly going out on a limb to cast him, yet I suspect he knew what he was doing, not only subverting the law, but combining two kinds of "other" into a single character, to borrow Bryan's terminology–blacks at the time being "other" to the police, and the police being "other" to the blacks. Which is where the grace comes in. It is perfect for

Maundy Thursday. (This excerpt is from NPR's Story Corps)

"I grew up in the ghetto. I did not have a positive opinion of police officers. Policeman were siccing police dogs and water hoses on people," he says. "And I really had a hard time putting myself in that role. So I was not excited about being Officer Clemmons at all." Still, Clemmons came around to it eventually and agreed to take on the role.

And, in the decades he spent as part of the show, there's one scene in particular that Clemmons remembers with great emotion. It was from an episode that aired in 1969, in which Rogers had been resting his feet in a plastic pool on a hot day.

> "He invited me to come over and to rest my feet in the water with him," Clemmons recalls. "The icon Fred Rogers not only was showing my brown skin in the tub with his white skin as two friends, but as I was getting out of that tub, he was helping me dry my feet."

He says he'll never forget the day Rogers wrapped up the program, as he always did, by hanging up his sweater and saying:

> "You make every day a special day just by being you, and I like you just the way you are." This time in particular, Rogers had been looking right at Clemmons, and after they wrapped he walked over. Clemmons asked him, "Fred, were you talking to me?"
>
> "Yes, I have been talking to you for years," Rogers said, as Clemmons recalls. "But you heard me today."
>
> "It was like telling me I'm OK as a human being," Clemmons says. "That was one of the most meaningful experiences I'd ever had."

Wow. There you have it. And before you cry Stuart Smalley, remember that Mr. Rogers was an ordained clergyman. As such, there's every reason to believe that he was coming from a place of conviction here re: what the Christian faith says about human identity. Not just that we ought to love our neighbor, but that the water of baptism cleans more than one's feet. As a result you are not who others see you to be, or who the law condemns you to be. You are not even who you see yourself to be. You are who God sees you to be, which is a forgiven sinner, a child of God, a son in whom he is well pleased.

The Prayer of St. Francis

Lord, make me an instrument of your peace:
where there is hatred, let me sow love;
where there is injury, pardon;
where there is doubt, faith;
where there is despair, hope;

where there is darkness, light;
where there is sadness, joy.
O divine Master, grant that I may not so much seek
to be consoled as to console,
to be understood as to understand,
to be loved as to love.
For it is in giving that we receive,
it is in pardoning that we are pardoned,
and it is in dying that we are born to eternal life.
Amen.

AFTER THE LAST SUPPER

Jen Rose Yokel[1]

The dirt mingled
in the water.
Three years' worth.

Even the traitor's.
Even the denier's.
(Already named at the table—
for there is no past,
present,
or future
in one who is
older than time.)

Peter resisted.
Would I have also?

Said no
to my king bowed low,
towel in hand,
wiping the dust
of the earth he owns?

The foot-worn
mud and grime
of past,
present,
and future
dissolve in
baptismal
waters.

FRIDAY

Robert Capon[1]

The Vaster End of Blood

In the Law of the Lord,
Leviticus, the eighth chapter, the fourteenth verse: Aaron
and his sons laying hands upon the bullock's head, blood
poured at the bottom of the altar to make reconciliation;
the caul above the liver, and the two kidneys and their
fat—all burnt by fire for a sweet savor.
Smoke, incense,
wave breast, heave shoulder, rams of consecration, the
pomegranate and the golden bell, sounding upon the
hem of the robe round about; priest and temple, death
and holocaust, always and everywhere.
Why?

It is tempting

simply to write it off as barbarism, nonsense, superstition;
to fault it and forget it;
But the fact of blood still stands,
reproving materialist and spiritualist at once; gainsaying
worlds too small and heavens too thin.
This superadded killing,
this sacrifice, these deaths which work no earthly inter-
change, this rich, imprudent waste
Witnesses
The City's undiminishable size:
Man wills to make of earth,
not one Jerusalem but two; this sacramental blood de-
clares the double mind by which he wills to lift both
lion and lamb beyond the killing to exchanges unaccount-
able and vast.
Man's priestliness therefore
bespeaks his refusal of despair; proclaims acceptance of
a world which, by its murderous hand, subscribes the
insupportable dilemma of its being—the war of lion and
lamb having no other likely outcome here than two im-
possibilities:
The one,
a pride of victors feeding on the slain; but leaving the
lion as he was before, trapped in ancient reciprocities by
which at last all power falls to crows;
And the other,
a hymn to despair no victim will accept; it is not enough,
in this paroxysm of martyrdoms, to stand upon the ship-
wrecks of the slain and praise the weak for weakness; the
lamb's will, too, was life; he died refusing death.
Sacrifice therefore
Not written off, but recognized,
a sign in blood of the vaster end of blood; a redness
turning all things white; an impossibility prefiguring the

last exchange of all.

The old order, of course,
unchanged; the deaths of bulls and goats achieving
nothing; Aaron still ineffectual; creation still bloody;
But haunted now by bells within the veil
where Aaron walks in shadows sprinkling
blood and bids a new Jerusalem descend.
Endless smoke now rising
Lion become priest
And lamb victim
The world awaits
The unimaginable union
By which the Lion lifts Himself Lamb slain
And, Priest and Victim,
Brings
The City
Home.

~ from Chapter 4 of Robert Farrar Capon's most
outstanding *The Supper of the Lamb*

WEEKEND

EVERY MOMENT HOLY

Tenebrae: A Liturgy for Those Who Weep Without Knowing Why

LEADER: There is so much lost in this world, O Lord,
so much that aches and groans and shivers
for want of redemption, so much that
seems dislocated, upended, desecrated,
unhinged—even in our own hearts.

PEOPLE: Even in our own hearts
we bear the mark of all that is broken.
What is best in this world has been bashed
and battered and trodden down.
What was meant to be the substance has
become the brittle shell, haunted by the
ghosts of a glory so long crumbled that only
its rubble is remembered now.

Is it any wonder we should weep sometimes,

without knowing why? It might be anything.
And then again, it might be everything.

For we feel this.
We who are your children feel
this empty space where some lost thing
should have rested in its perfection,
and we pine for those nameless glories,
and we pine for all the wasted stories in our world,
and we pine for these present wounds.
We pine for our children and for their children too,
knowing each will have to prove how this universal pain is
also personal. We pine for all children born into these days
of desolation—
whose regal robes were torn to tatters before they were even
swaddled in them.

O Lord, how can we not weep,
when waking each day in this vale of tears?
How can we not feel those pangs,
when we, wounded by others,
so soon learn to wound as well,
and in the end wound even ourselves?
We grieve what we cannot heal and
we grieve our half-belief,
having made uneasy peace with disillusion,
aligning ourselves with a self-protective lie
that would have us kill our best hopes
just to keep our disappointments half-confined.

We feel ourselves wounded by what is wretched,
foul, and fell,
but we are sometimes wounded by the beauty as well,
for when it whispers,

it whispers of the world
that might have been our birthright,
now banished,
now withdrawn,
as unreachable to our wounded hearts
as ancient seas receding down
some endless dark.

We weep, O Lord,
for those things that,
though nameless, are still lost.
We weep for the cost of our rebellions,
for the mocking and hollowing of holy things,
for the inward curve of our souls,
for the evidences of death outworked in
every field and tree and blade of grass,
crept up in every creature, alert in every
longing, infecting all fabrics of life.

We weep for the leers our daughters will endure,
as if to be made in reflection of your beauty
were a fault for which they must pay.
We weep for our sons,
sabotaged by profiteers who seek to warp their dreams
before they even come of age.

We weep for all the twisted alchemies of our times
that would turn what might have been gold
into crowns of cheap tin
and then toss them into refuse bins
as if love could ever be
a castoff thing one might simply be done with.
We weep for the wretched expressions of all things
that were first built of goodness and glory

but are now their own shadow twins.
We have wept so often.
And we will weep again.

And yet, there is somewhere in our tears
a hope still kept.

We feel it in this darkness,
like a tiny flame,
when we are told

Jesus also wept.

You wept.

So moved by the pain of this crushed creation,
you, O Lord, heaved with the grief of it,
drinking the anguish like water
and sweating it out of your skin like blood.

Is it possible that you—in your sadness
over Lazarus, in your grieving for
Jerusalem, in your sorrow in the garden—
is it possible that you have sanctified
our weeping too?

For the grief of God is no small thing,
and the weeping of God is not without effect.
The tears of Jesus preceded
a resurrection of the dead.

O Spirit of God,
is it then possible
that our tears might also be

a kind of intercession?

That we, your children, in our groaning
with the sadness of creation, could
be joining in some burdened work
of coming restoration? Is it possible
that when we weep and don't know why,
it is because the curse has ranged
so far, so wide? That we weep at that
which breaks your heart, because it
has also broken ours—sometimes so deeply
that we cannot explain our weeping,
even to ourselves?

If that is true,
then let such weeping be received, O Lord,
as an intercession newly forged of holy sorrow.

Then let our tears anoint these broken things,
and let our grief be as their consecration—
a preparation for their promised
redemption, our sorrow sealing them
for that day when you will take
the ache of all creation,
and turn it inside-out,
like the shedding of
an old gardener's glove.

ALL: O Lord, if it please you,
when your children weep
and don't know why,
yet use our tears
to baptize what you love.

Amen.[1]

Desdichado, Dorothy Sayers

—This is the heir; come let us kill him.

—Who is this that cometh up from the wilderness, leaning on her Beloved?

Christ walks the world again, His lute upon His back,
His red robe rent to tatters, His riches gone to rack,
The wind that wakes the morning blows His hair about His face,
His hands and feet are ragged with the ragged briar's embrace,
For the hunt is up behind Him and His sword is at His side,
...
Christ the bonny outlaw walks the whole world wide,
Singing: "Lady, lady, will you come away with Me,
Lie among the bracken and break the barley bread?
We will see new suns arise in golden, far-off skies,
For the Son of God and Woman hath not where to lay His head."

Christ walks the world again, a prince of fairy-tale,
He roams, a rascal fiddler, over mountain and down dale,
Cast forth to seek His fortune in a bitter world and grim,
For the stepsons of His Father's house would steal His bride from Him;
They have weirded Him to wander till He bring within His hands
The water of eternal youth from black-enchanted lands,

Singing: "Lady, lady, will you come away with Me,
Or sleep on silken cushions in the bower of wicked men?
For if we walk together through the wet and windy weather,
When I ride back home triumphant, you will ride beside
Me then."

Christ walks the world again, new-bound on high emprise,
With music in His golden mouth and laughter in His eyes;
The primrose springs before Him as He treads the
dusty way,
His singer's crown of thorns has burst in blossom like
the may,
He heedeth not the morrow and He never looks behind,
Singing: "Glory to the open skies and peace to all mankind."

Singing: "Lady, lady, will you come away with Me?
Was never man lived longer for the hoarding of his breath;
Here be dragons to be slain, here be rich rewards to gain . . .
If we perish in the seeking . . . why, how small a thing is
death!"

WEEK EIGHT

PRACTICING RESURRECTION

Justin Edgar

What does it mean to practice resurrection. Cue Eugene
Peterson:

> *The church is an appointed gathering of named people in*
> *particular places who practice a life of resurrection in a*
> *world where death gets the biggest headlines: death of*
> *nations, death of civilization, death of marriage, death of*
> *careers, obituaries without end. Death by war, death by*
> *murder, death by accident, death by starvation. Death by*
> *electric chair, lethal injection, hanging. The practice of*
> *resurrection is the intentional, deliberate decision to*
> *believe and participate in the resurrection life, life out of*
> *death, life that trumps death, life that is the last word,*
> *Jesus life. This practice is not a vague wish upwards but*
> *comprises a number of discrete but interlocking acts that*

maintain a credible and faithful way of life. Real life, in a world preoccupied with death and the devil.

These practices include the worship of God in all the operations of the Trinity: the acceptance of the resurrection, born-from-above identify in baptism; the embrace of resurrection formation by eating and drinking Christ's resurrection body and blood at the Lord's Table; attentive reading of and obedience to the revelation of God in the Scripture; prayer that cultivates an intimacy with realities that are inaccessible to our senses; confession and forgiveness of sins; welcoming the stranger and outcast; working and speaking for peace and justice, healing and truth, sanctity and beauty; care for creation. The practice of resurrection encourages improvisation on the basic resurrection story as given in our Scriptures and revealed in Jesus. Thousands of derivative unanticipated resurrection details proliferate the landscape. The company of people who practice resurrection replicates the way of Jesus on the highways and byways named and numbered on all the maps of the world...this is the church...it is an open invitation to live eternity in time.[1]

During this first week of Easter, I thought it important to pause, and think about how we are aimed and shaped toward resurrection life. These practices that we have discussed together are all practices linked to the resurrection life of Jesus. And that is our script by the way. Our script is His resurrected life. We engage in these practices, so that our imaginations may be captured by that story, by that reality. We are animated by it. Like actors on the stage, but the production is a practice improv. We prep and prepare, studying lines and scenarios, and then as we know who we are, we are unleashed to the stage. While on the stage our imaginations have been formed and we know the script to such a degree that we can improv God's action in the world. This is what it means to practice resurrection. All the world is a stage, and we are the actors. God is our audience and our muse. We have a script of the Scriptures and practices that have made us the actors we are, and now we are unleashed into the performance of our lives, filled with blessings, songs, singing, confessions, creeds, bread, wine, water, enemies and neighbors, justice, mercy, generosity, dance and mission, and through our acting, all the world will be blessed, eternity will seep into time.

MONDAY

COLOSSIANS 3:1-14

Jeremy Warren

In today's culture, the crux of our identity naturally comes out of what we DO. I am a teacher, graphic designer, father, ultimate frisbee lover. Or I am an engineer. Or a firefighter, or a mother, or a counselor, or an architect, or a realtor... We find who we are in what occupies the bulk of our time. It hardly seems wrong to think this way. Especially since we grew up with the burning question: "what do you want to BE when you grow up?" So simple, and yet, it can be so damaging to our comprehension of who we actually are as Christians. I love this quote from a theologian and professor, Marcus Johnson: "All the rights and privileges of being the children of God are conveyed to us in our union with God's own Son, a union that Paul thinks of in the most intimate and profoundly real ways. In our union with the person of Christ in salvation, we share in his personal relationship to the Father and the glorious benefits that attend that relationship: we are co-heirs with Christ, we can cry to the Father as Jesus did, the Father loves us as he loves his own Son, the Father hears our prayers, and more. God does not just think of us *as if* we were his children; we *are* his children through our participation in his Son." In salvation, we become a new being. We attain a new identity, which justifies what Paul says to the Corinthians (2 Cor. 5:17) that we are "a *new creation*. The old has passed away; behold, the new has come."

Wait, so I am not just what I do? As we see in Colossians, Paul takes us into series of connections between who we truly are (or who we truly were) and what actions we are supposed to live into (or run away from) to rightly walk in our new and beautiful identity. When I read this, it's almost as if the pressure valve is released. All the built up cultural pressure to be the best teacher or designer, or whatever I DO, does not make me who I am at the end of the day. If have a hard day, that does not mean that I am not good at what I do and consequently have to question my place in life. But I will have hard days and great days; and in that I can fully worship God in my resurrection because he has gifted me with great and perfect skills and gifts. I can let my life be a spiritual act of worship as I do what I enjoy and what I have been trained to do. And the underlying person behind my skills is a righteous, holy, saved individual intimately wrapped up into the person of Christ.

All the time we have access to God, the ability to commune with Him and His Body because we are linked together in Christ. Likewise, we have the ability to worship together before God because we are brought into the same fold/flock/family. We can daily practice resurrection because we have been brought into a similar process of new life just as Jesus experienced three days after the Cross. We can celebrate the resurrection of Christ in a new light because that is the miracle we are living every single day! Hallelujah! We are made new and we have been given detailed guidance from Paul (and of course the Holy Spirit) of how to practically walk in our new identity. Our identity is made known to the world through these actions - not our day job, our familial position of a father, mother, or child, or even our greatest accomplishments.

Father, help me to daily find my identity in your Son and not in what I do. Draw me close every hour and allow me to worship you with the skills you have given me. Allow me strength and wisdom, Lord as I seek to listen and follow your instruction that you have given through your inspired Word. As your adopted child, will you help me to trust in the person you have made me through your Son Jesus Christ. I pray this in the name of the Father, The Son, and The Holy Spirit, Amen.

TUESDAY

PHILIPPIANS 3:8-11

Joanna Hinks

Countless resources abound, in books, seminars, online, etc., to teach us how to practice the "victorious Christian life". Based on this passage of Scripture, I think the Apostle Paul would have tossed most of those in the garbage. How does he describe it? In terms of loss and suffering. The loss of all the things that made up his own righteousness, and sharing in the suffering and even the death of Christ.

That's not something I'm comfortable pondering. While I joyfully embrace the Gospel of grace on Sunday morning, my day-to-day actions tend to emphasize my own efforts and I really like to take credit for my successes. It's a struggle to embrace the attitude of loss - loss of pride, loss of control. And like most people, I would do almost anything to avoid suffering.

But it's not MY victory that I should be seeking, nor MY resurrection. Paul desperately seeks to be found in Christ -

to forsake his own previous identity as a keeper of the law and be identified so closely with Christ that he experiences Christ's resurrection. That loss and death of self is the very foundation of Christian victory.

Jesus, help me to give up my own righteousness that I so tenaciously cling to. Give me the courage to joyfully share in your suffering and death. Teach me to find victory in your victory and new life in your resurrection.

WEDNESDAY

2 TIMOTHY 2:1-13

Joshua Spare

I remember the first time that I realized just how much was changing in having children. It was the night before my son was born, as I sat on the floor outside the room in which my wife was getting her epidural, having already labored fruitlessly for 9 hours. I was exhausted (this is not a comparison to anything that my wife was going through, simply a mere statement of how tired I was!), and I was enjoying a small reprieve in the form of the most delicious bowl of Chipotle that I had ever eaten. As I leaned my head back against the wall, I thought, "I can't wait until this is over!" And almost immediately, the absurdity of the statement crashed down upon my head!

I have stayed up late many, many nights in my life—I'm a pernicious procrastinator, and there have been countless philosophy papers or biology labs finished in the wee hours of the morning, when most people are just starting to rouse from their slumber. I recall the physical agony of forcing myself to class on 15 minutes of shut-eye, thinking, "just get through the class, and then you can nap!" As I sat there in the L&D ward, I thought, "just a bit longer, and then I can nap!" How silly! How absurd! The tiredness was just beginning; the sleeplessness was in its infancy!

I have thought back to that moment many times in my short tenure as a parent; it was the moment that everything shifted in my mind and categorically altered my thinking about "my time." In a similar vein, I see Paul exhorting Timothy to think upon the resurrection in similar terms: "Timothy, remember the resurrection! Remember Jesus who was buried and is resurrected! Think how this changed *everything*!" Because of the resurrection, Paul is willing to endure all manner of torture and imprisonment. Because of the resurrection, we have salvation. Because of the resurrection, we have eternal joy in Christ!

Moreover, we have been resurrected with Christ - we were buried in our sins and trespasses, but washed clean in the blood of Christ and raised to new life in Christ! We are the resurrection! And in all of this, Paul is telling Timothy: "Remember the resurrection! Everything, *everything*, has changed because of Christ risen! Now go and tell others who will be so transformed that they will tell others in turn!"

Jesus, please help me to remember your resurrection; please give me eyes to see how everything has been altered in light of the resurrection, and give me words to tell of the joy of life in your resurrection!

THURSDAY

ROMANS 8:31-39

Angela Breidenbach

As a missionary to the former Soviet bloc nations, Romans 8:31-39 has become one of my "go to" sections of scripture. In a part of the world where Christianity was outlawed, and punishable by death, for over three generations, there is a palpable spiritual darkness that the devil loves to feed on, and we often find ourselves under attack. One of the reasons that I love these verses is because they lend themselves to literally any situation in which we, as Christians, can find ourselves...from day to day trials to full out spiritual warfare.

To that end, I often refer to them as the "fill in the blank" scripture, and our teams sometimes practice putting whatever is troubling us into the list of things that cannot separate us from the love of Christ. To be sure, this is a comforting thing, but if we fail to consider the way in which God conquered the devil and all of his forces, these verses are no more or less than many of the spiritual mantras that can be found in a myriad of self-help resources in any bookstore or internet site. To fully understand the power of these verses, it is important to look closely at the beginning of verse 32 specifically, which says: He who did not spare his own Son but gave him up for us all. As humankind, we simply cannot begin to fathom the kind of love that it took to be nailed to the cross with the sins of all humanity holding Jesus there. It was only through that act, that Jesus opened the kingdom of heaven for all who believe, and it is only through His glorious resurrection that we can live in the sure and certain hope that *nothing* in all of creation can separate us from the love of God in Christ Jesus our Lord!

Thank you, Lord, for your love that we cannot be separated from - love that is better than life itself.

FRIDAY

THE EASTER EFFECT, DOLLY PARTON, AND A
SPECIFIC KIND OF JESUS

Bryan J[1]

Happy Easter! By now, the ham leftovers should be about finished, the bonnets returned to their boxes, and the elusive eggs left unfound on Sunday are easily discovered by following the faint smell of sulfur. Clergy are just about recovered from the multiple services of Holy Week. And for those of us from liturgical traditions, Alleluias are back on the table. Lent has passed, and we're now in an "Easter State of Mind."

That "Easter State of Mind" is the subject of one of the better think-pieces offered up by the web this year. At the Wall Street Journal, George Weigel gives a half-history lesson, half-apologetic for the Resurrection.

There is no accounting for the rise of Christianity without weighing the revolutionary effect on those nobodies of what they called "the Resurrection": their encounter with the one whom they embraced as the Risen Lord, whom they first knew as the itinerant Jewish rabbi, Jesus of Nazareth, and who died an agonizing and shameful death on a Roman cross outside Jerusalem. As N.T. Wright, one of the Anglosphere's pre-eminent biblical scholars, makes clear, that first generation answered the question of why they were Christians with a straightforward answer: because Jesus was raised from the dead...

This remarkable and deliberate recording of the first Christians' incomprehension of what they insisted was the irreducible bottom line of their faith teaches us two things. First, it tells us that the early Christians were confident enough about what they called the Resurrection that (to borrow from Prof. Wright) they were prepared to say something like, "I know this sounds ridiculous, but it's what happened." And the second thing it tells us is that it took time for the first Christians to figure out what the events of Easter meant—not only for Jesus but for themselves. As they worked that out, their thinking about a lot of things changed profoundly...

The article mentions three positive secular outcomes brought to the ancient world through Christianity—an increased dignity given to woman in contrast to the classical culture, a self-denying healthcare provided to plague sufferers, and a focus on family health and growth. Weigel suggests that it's only through an Easter State of Mind, what he calls the Easter Effect, that these benefits make sense. This set of actions performed by early Christians only makes sense if people actually believe in Jesus's resurrection.

Weigel goes on to suggest that this "Easter Effect" changed more than just behaviors that benefited the ancient secular culture. It changed the way people thought about time and history, their responsibilities to their neighbor, their worship and temporal rhythms, and even their relationship with the idea of resurrection itself. Early Christians are changing their sabbath days to Sundays, inviting new members into their religion, embracing persecution and death, and living as if they knew the outcome of history itself. The social changes that followed Good Friday, documented in both Bible and history, make the most sense if the people engaging in them actually believed in the resurrection of Jesus.

All these things are good and true, and it's a good thing this conversation is happening in a national publication. There's an addendum worth adding to the article which helps make its case, and it comes from an unexpected source. The greatest Easter anthem ever composed was not written by Bach or Handel. It's Dolly Parton's version of *He's Alive,* a retelling of The Resurrection from Peter's point of view. The third verse in particular is a work of theological depth—John and Peter have heard about the empty tomb, they've run out to see it, and now they've returned home.

Back inside the house again
The guilt and anguish came
Everything I'd promised Him
Just added to my shame
When at last it came to choices
I denied I knew His name
And even if He was alive
It wouldn't be the same

Peter, of course, is famous for boasting of his devotion to Jesus on Thursday and denying him three times before

Friday got out of bed. And the great insight of the song is that The Resurrection could very well have been the world's most terrifying event. The risen Jesus could have come back with vengeance on his mind, now immortal and ready to carry out a war against the Romans and Sanhedrin. The risen Jesus could have returned with a host of angel soldiers and began his Final Judgment that very Sunday morning. The risen Jesus could have found Peter and had a "come to Jesus" conversation about the denials, expelling him as a disciple. Peter isn't just worried about Roman soldiers, he's now worried about facing up to the Jesus he denied a few days prior.

Reading the resurrection stories in the gospels, there are plenty of themes that the four authors want to emphasize. One among them is that the resurrection was a bodily resurrection—scars were preserved, fish was digested, hands were placed in wounds. Another is that the resurrection was an embarrassment to worldly powers, with heavy stones moved, Roman soldiers terrified, and religious authorities spreading cover-up propaganda. Equally as important to the story, however, is that The Resurrection is an act of divine love to the undeserved. Jesus appears to weeping women, terrified men, doubters, runaways, people who don't know their bibles, and disciples who quit the business and went back to their day jobs. It's almost as if a qualification for meeting with the resurrected Jesus is being a really bad disciple of Jesus.

Which is to say, The Resurrection isn't just that someone rose from the dead. The reanimation of Lazarus didn't inspire a women's rights movement, nor did the resuscitation of the Rabbi's daughter inspire a generation of self-emptying plague doctors. The good news is that the one who rose from the dead is, specifically and uniquely, Jesus of Nazareth, friend of sinners, love incarnate, son of God, and full of grace. It's this particular Jesus that caused the disciples to reconsider time and space and Sabbath, and also, love and forgiveness and the entire nature of the divine. Replace this Jesus with anyone else, and the whole movement falls flat.

The news doesn't get much better than that on Easter.

NOTES

Week One

1. *Calhoun, Rebecca. "On Keeping Lent." Resurrection Brooklyn, 12 Feb. 2018, resurrectionbrooklyn.org/on-keeping-lent/.*
2. *Ibid.*

Thursday

1. Timothy Keller, *The Songs of Jesus: a Year of Daily Devotions in the Psalms.* Viking, 2015.

Week Two

1. Justin Whitmel Earley, *The Common Rule: Habits of Purpose for an Age of Distraction,* InterVarsity Press, 2019.

Weekend Reflection

1. Will Willimon, "Good News! You're a Sinner and Lent Is Here." OnFaith, 17 Feb. 2015, www.onfaith.co/onfaith/2014/03/02/good-news-you-are-a-sinner-and-lent-is-here/31125.

Weekend Reflection

1. CJ Green, "Lessons from the Mid-Lent Slump." Mockingbird, 25 Feb. 2019, mbird.com/2018/03/lessons-from-the-mid-lent-slump/?highlight=lent.

Week Four

1. David Foster Wallace, *This Is Water: Some Thoughts, Delivered on a Significant Occasion about Living a Compassionate Life.* Little, Brown, 2009.

Weekend Reflection

1. Sarah Condon. "What Would Jesus Do (for Lent)?" Mockingbird, 22 Feb. 2016, mbird.com/2015/02/what-would-jesus-do-for-lent/?highlight=What%2Bwould%2BJesus%2BDo%2B%28for%2BLent%29.

Friday

1. *Powers, Adam. "The Magicians Nephew: Singing Creation Into Being." Thepublicans.org, 14 Oct. 2013, thepublicans.org/2013/10/14/the-magicians-nephew-singing-creation-into-being/.*

Weekend Reflection

1. Reggie Kidd, "Bach, Bubba and the Blues Brothers ." Bach, Bubba, and the Blues Brothers: The Singing Saviors Many Voices - Dr. Reggie Kidd, 1999, rq.rts.edu/summer99/kidd.html.

Week Six

1. Smith, James K. A. *Desiring the Kingdom: Worship, Worldview, and Cultural Formation.* Baker Academic, 2011.

Weekend

1. Andrew Peterson, "The Rabbit Room." The Rabbit Room Theres No Right or Wrong In Art Comments, 16 Apr. 2017, rabbitroom.com/2017/04/holy-week-sonnets/.

Thursday

1. David Zahl, "Maundy Thursday Miscellany: Mr Rogers, Stinky Feet, Memes, Cartoons, and Jams, plus Love & Friendship!" Mockingbird, 25 Mar. 2016, mbird.com/2016/03/maundy-thursday-miscellany-mr-rogers-god-of-stinky-feet-memes-cartoons-and-jams-plus-love-friendship-trailer/?highlight=mr%2Brogers.

After The Last Supper

1. Jen Rose Yokel, "The Rabbit Room." The Rabbit Room Theres No Right or Wrong In Art Comments, 24 Mar. 2016, rabbitroom.com/2016/03/after-the-last-supper/.

Friday

1. Robert Capon, "The Rabbit Room." The Rabbit Room Theres No Right or Wrong In Art Comments, 25 Mar. 2015, rabbitroom.com/2016/03/the-vaster-end-of-blood/.

Weekend

1. Douglas McKelvey, "A LITURGY FOR THOSE WHO Weep Without Knowing Why." The Rabbit Room , 28 Mar. 2018, rabbit-room.com/2018/03/for-tenebrae-a-liturgy-for-those-who-weep-without-knowing-why/.

Week Eight

1. Eugene H. Peterson, *Practice Resurrection: a Conversation on Growing up in Christ.* William B. Eerdmans Publishing, 2013, Amazon, www.amazon.com/Practice-Resurrection-Conversation-Petersons-Conversations/dp/0802869327/ref=sr_1_1?crid=10VI8QXE1T5ME&keywords=practice+resurrection+eugene+peterson&qid=1551287669&s=gateway&sprefix=practice+res%2Caps%2C156&sr=8-1.

Friday

1. Bryan J, "The Easter Effect, Dolly Parton, and a Specific Kind of Jesus." Mockingbird, 23 July 2018, www.mbird.com/2018/04/the-easter-effect-dolly-parton-and-a-specific-kind-of-jesus/.